Knud Holscher

Contents

Poul Erik Skriver

Knud Holscher

Architect and Industrial Designer

with an introduction by
Poul Erik Tøjner

Edition Axel Menges

© 2000 Edition Axel Menges, Stuttgart/London
ISBN 3-930698-79-X

Reproductions: Bild und Text Baun, Fellbach
Printing and binding: Daehan Printing and Publishing Co., Ltd., Sungnam, Korea

Translation into English: Courtney D. Coyne
Layout: Knud Holscher, Birgitte Redin and Jens Christian Larsen

Lucca
Duomo
96 heves.
ped

Architecture or art
Poul Erik Tøjner

I. Architects have to set human and social relationships in relief; they provide them with a face, an expressive mode and a corresponding framework. The modern world has compromised the unity of the age-old conceptions of the good the true and the beautiful in many ways, hence disabling them as a regulating idea. But this has not prevented modern architecture from keeping up with ethics, politics and aesthetics. By starting from here, we can establish a vision of architecture that can resemble a vision of life to a striking degree.

One might assume that the incredibly comprehensive and diversified practice of the Danish architect and designer Knud Holscher is not based on any vision of architecture at first sight. One is immediately ware of intense activity conducted at a dizzying pace, apparently devoid of a general outlook. It might seem that he has always grasped at everything and anything that has come within his reach. This is evident from the time he started work in. Arne Jacobsen's small design studio in Copenhagen, via his experience as a partner and key figure in the office of Krohn & Hartvig Rasmussen Architects, up to the present day, where he presides over his own successful practice, Knud Holscher Industrial Design. This book, for instance, illustrates an impressively broad range of work extending from universities to doorknobs, from Arabian museums to toilet bowls, from office landscape planning to coffee pots and from bus stop shelters to concrete building elements.

Nevertheless, appearances can be deceptive. There is a Danish saying that means "After a spreader come a gatherer", and within the work of Knud Holscher there has always been a power to gather that is present from conception to completion. This power and strength stems from his vision of architecture, and the multiplicity and versatility of his production fosters continuity; he focuses, he does not blur.

Spreading is the keyword. Holscher's outlook on architecture specifically expresses that design is something that extends through many things, that is present in many things. It is almost a dimension in its own right. It is not to be reserved for privileged niches of society nor for specific aesthetic realms of life. Architecture and design ought to develop in relation to everyday life and to daily existence just as nature evolves in accordance with its own functions and conditions.

II. Holscher's vision of architecture says, in other words, that everything deserves thoughtfully considered design. Nothing is too small, too humble or too modest to be designed. Design is a fundamental human activity that implies our inherent alienation in the world – we are not merely natural. It expresses our individual nature and our desire to adapt ourselves to the world, and the world to ourselves.

Alienation and adaptability are commensurate parts of the creative impulse that stimulate the production of architecture. Our alienation compels us to intervene in the world with our own designs, which did not previously exist in the natural world. No architect could possibly disagree with this. However, there have been architects throughout the ages who have exploited this knowledge and created an essentially totalitarian design program, to be imposed on everything. Caricatured functionalism can be such a program, sometimes functionalistic designs are not generated solely from their functions, but beforehand, as an abstract idea.

Alienation must counter-balance adaptability's sensitivity to the world. Temptation towards ideals must be countered by being open to solutions derived from concrete situations and concrete objects. Knud Holscher's vision of architecture is based on these two fundamental insights, as well as on an understanding that alienation and adaptability are reciprocal, leading both to both diversity and continuity in his work. All of his designs may manifest themselves differently, though they consistently respond to the same concrete questions.

Holscher's architecture and design derive from this tension between conception and execution. His work has never involved merely putting ideas into action. It is more like a process of fusing and welding these two spheres to encompass one another. This makes him an architect; an architect grounded in the everyday world. He is an architect who

respects the concrete practicality of everyday life and reveres it as the most meaningful challenge to the profession.

Oddly enough, it is these same qualities that set him at odds with much of the architecture of the last few decades – architecture that, to a large degree, has courted art more than everyday things. Holscher's work can be seen as a firm statement in a discussion concerning modern life and the formation of its objects and aspirations. His designs also address the aesthetics of modern art and its dominant influence on empirical development and the formation of ideals at the end of the century. What then do these experiences reveal, especially in terms of the formation of ideals?

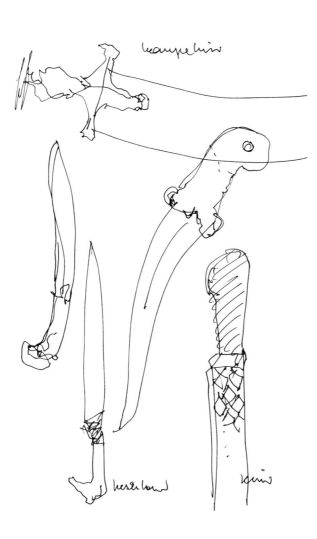

III. We have learned that in principle there is nothing that binds modern humanity. Life is noncommittal and free. However, in return for this freedom we can no longer attach ourselves to anything. We have learned this painfully. This is the price of freedom.

Modern art shows us the formula for this freedom. Modern art is unbound; it is there to break rules and to bear freedom as its own watermark. It consequently sounds a melancholy note because it is unable to hide the price of its freedom: loss of perspective, loss of coherence, loss of reality.

It is even more paradoxical that the majority of modern art strives to be more real than reality. This is the dream. However, it is modern art's own freedom that prevents this dream from coming to fruition. The price of freedom is unfortunately a certain loss of reality. Modern art is often unreal or overreal. Modern art is just that – art.

Modern art is there to make a difference, but simply as art. It appeals to a reality where it can operate as art, as something different from the other forces that plague its reality. Whether on the market or in museums, it is art's conditions of freedom, mobility and change that simultaneously govern its existence and threaten its impacting force. Modern art is at odds with reality, yet it wants to be part of reality at the same time. Modern art longs to be both free and indispensable. This is not a minor wish, and it is not easy to meet.

Architecture is a form of art. Classical architecture is a part of Classical art, whilst modern architecture is a part of modern art. But this is not as simple as it may seem. Architecture is heir to an ancient inheritance that includes both the dream and the threat of modern art. This dream is there to make a difference. It wishes to change the world into something new and different through the artwork's intervention. This remains a dream. Perhaps the century's most persistent one.

Expanding this discourse, the French sociologist, Jean Baudrillard cynically states: "When I go to the Biennales or see FIAC exhibitions at the Grand Palais I am confronted by the total and colossal global uselessness of art. I cannot imagine what kind of dramatic role art could play in the evolution of the world." Furthering this notion in his book *Cool Memories*, he writes: "Le retour automatique du chariot de la machine à écrire, la fermeture, centrale, électronique des quatre portes de la voiture, ca c'est des choses qui comptent. Le reste n'est que théorie et litérature." "The automatic typewriter carriage return, the electronic, central locking system for the car doors, these are the omit things that count. The rest is just theory and literature."

IV. Architecture, on the other hand, does make a difference. Perhaps it does not play a leading role in the evolution of the world but it has earned itself some kind of role. It manifests itself as massive and permanent; it can be brutal or elegant, forceful or inconspicuous. Regardless of its formation, architecture does make a material impact. It maintains space as public matter despite modernity's constant affinity with the private. One is reasonably free to choose to view, read or listen to art. Buildings, though, are static and enduring entities that are relatively impossible to ignore and avoid. Architecture dictates to material – with some modifications.

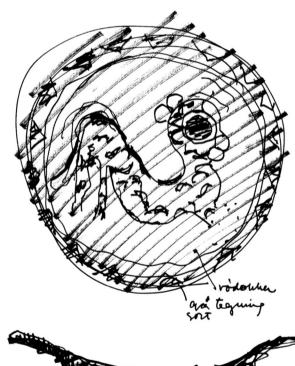

Seen from the vantage point of modern art, the nightmare is architecture's responsibilities in reality. Architecture is not a free form of art but is finite. It is limited by its function and purpose. It is bound by its own being. Understood as such, architecture is completely incongruous with modern aesthetics. There is no point in seeking deeper insight into the essence of modern art. Nowhere in modern art can one find a reflection on architecture's being. Instead one finds confrontation after confrontation. May be modern architecture does not exist as a form of art after all.

Scanning the last few decades of architecture, it could seem that architecture's most honourable task has been to convince its observers that modern architecture does exist – as art. Perhaps instead of discussing architecture's essence and ancient inheritance – its functional dimension – one should speak of an ancient debt; a debt that should be settled immediately for the sake of the profession's ambitions and claims.

Both deconstructive and narrative architecture attempt to emancipate themselves from their obligations through rhetorical theorizing, amateur philosophy and aesthetic glamour. In short, architecture is transformed into an abstract spatial discourse that amalgamates design and history. Put even more precisely, this kind of "architecturing" seeks to join modern art through the aesthetic principles of modern art. It wants to be independent now, but at the same time indispensable. It desires to be as visionary and radical as its contemporaries. It longs to be the spirit of time, disguised as the spirit of place.

25/12 97 hn. Indianer market San Christobal

There is nothing new about architects manœuvring and orienting themselves within a sphere of design and history. Our designs are infused with history. Great architects and great architectural epochs have made their impact and then left it to us to carry the heritage and the debt. It has always been like this. Art, in a broad sense, creates a communicative space with a peripheral view to other forms of art. It transpires at a distance, under self-imposed isolation or under the pretence of perfecting a project.

This fairly non-controversial interplay with the other art forms and with its predecessors and colleagues is just one side of the traditional relationship. One could perhaps call it the social side. People relate to one another in space and time. Architects do this as well. In modern times, though, there is also an ideological side to the relationship. Artists reflect upon the histories closest to their own time. They formulate opinions and take stances in response to the previous

schools' doctrines and strategies. They are intent on superseding their antecedents or at least placing their emphasis elsewhere. After all, no one wants to repeat something that already exists.

This ideological aspect is one of modern art's most important inspirations. It is nothing new because "new" is merely a refinement in the manner in which art breaks free. It exclusively defines itself and its own circles, opposing the other arts and the codes governing them. Here, aesthetics' mirror image indicates the extreme of the theory and architecture, as a form of art, expires. Not surprisingly, practitioners of this theory would protest, identifying this as the point where architecture begins to be art. If this is correct, then should one not at least be willing to agree that this is also the point where architecture ceases to be architecture?

Various questions then arise: to what degree has the architecture of the last few decades been sacrificed as a

result of its dream of emancipation; a dream about architecture's inherent rule, its identity and its self-definition? After architecture's extroverted and often visionary life in the preceding decades, has it now turned inward, against itself? Has architecture abandoned its obligations and with them the possibility of making a difference – as a form of art?

Actually, it is something of a catastrophe. Building activity continues regardless. Nonetheless, if architects fail to retain building as the nucleus of their art form then they stand to lose more than just their historical justification. Even more tragically, we could lose our landmarks.

V. Obviously, if art is perceived from its deepest origins, than there is little sense in calling Knud Holscher an anti-aesthetic architect. Therefore, I define "art" as the unruly trade that compromises its origins daily through the Western World's commodification of spirit. Furthermore, if one associates anti-aesthetics with a critique of beauty and form, then it becomes completely meaningless. An anti-aesthetic practice is not the same as a non-aesthetic practice. Hence, there is good reason to maintain that Holscher is an anti-aesthetic architect owing to the distinct advantage of a self-restrained conception of architecture. Holscher gives precedence to sustaining the discipline of architecture within a central position between current technological problem solving and a future-oriented functional dimension.

According to Holscher, it is necessary to accept new technology. Quite simply, it is the tool that is available. The transformation from the tradition-bound craftsman's society – that of Holscher's upbringing – to our current, radical, mobile and perpetually progressive society is a fait accompli. This is regrettable, as it provides insurmountable problems for society's institutions during its transitional phases. It doesn't make any sense for a modern architect to avoid or attempt to elude these problems.

Conversely, what does make sense is careful attention to objects and time. This lies in the original ethos of the craft tradition, in the sense of a work's meanings and intentions. This concern manifests itself in Holscher; in his concrete resource-consciousness, in his economical and ecological concerns and, lastly, in his adherence to the understanding that architects do not raise monuments for lives that have been lived, but create foundations for the lives of the future.

At first glance, the design of the Cernova toilet for IFÖ, with a hidden drain trap and a joint above the seat, between the cistern and the bowl, might seem only a modest part of Holscher's design. And yet it is an almost perfect illustration of how innovative thinking can act as a major impetus for design. The toilet's form derives from the intention to alleviate and reduce thousands of hours of future cleaning work. Other comparable examples worth mentioning are the Quinta spotlights for ERCO. They too were chiefly designed based on considerations for a future-oriented functional dimension. Each spotlight has an integrated sextant and compass that enables settings to be programmed and reprogrammed. This feature is especially useful in museums and public spaces where it ensures that the appropriate lighting levels are achieved and maintained.

VI. The two extremes are the actual problem solving and the concern for the functional quality of the product's future. They provide definite focal points in the ellipse surrounding Holscher's architectonic logic, his sense of order and repetitive motifs, and his sense of the necessary and sufficient spirituality in a product. The challenge, thus, is constant. Whether it is an industrial design element or a building, the design cannot be liberated to the status of an image without sacrificing its functional reality.

Anti-aesthetic architecture could also be defined as a critique of architecture as image. Can one then view Knud Holscher's architecture as one such critique of images? Can his architecture be seen as a critique of visual hegemony in our culture?

If so, then how? A house is, of course, also an image – just ask anyone with the slightest interest in architecture. The answer is simple: architecture possesses an unavoidable visual or pictorial dimension, but its deciding philosophical point is that it is non-pictorial in its spatiality. Clever theorists would probably claim that architecture's three-dimensional quality is just a beautiful realization of a two-dimensional image's dream of becoming reality. Well, they are mistaken. Images are images and buildings are buildings. A space is not an image unfolded into its third dimension. A space relates to our physicality, and structures the concrete, whilst images operate mainly in our imaginations. Cyberspace and Post-Modern computer philosophy share

the goal of simulating the body and space into an image. It is precisely here then that architecture can make its presence known, build its walls and maintain its power of resistance.

The architectonic critique of the image's precedence in our culture is manifested in the largest and the smallest of Holscher's creations. It lies in his fundamental ethic vis-à-vis his work. It is a guiding principle right down to the last detail, such as the manner in which Holscher presents his designs. Diverse sales and marketing materials are graphically designed by Holscher himself and reveal the architect's special aptitude and proclivity for the image's logic instead of its seduction.

Right down to the graphic details, one senses Holscher's position between self-worshipping, artistic architects and experts in art-design. On one side there are drawings that may be regarded as philosophy drafted with ruler and compass. On the other side are advanced, back-lit photos in fragmental displays that endow consumer products with a spiritual appeal, transforming them into relics of aesthetics' new religion.

Conversely, Holscher's presentations are simple and refined. The pictorial aspect of the architecture or design is not denied, but is made as a clear representation of the logic that has guided the production. This is evident in all his works ranging from Odense University's distinctive arrangement based on the combination of squares to the d-line series' infinite variations based on a given concept. Holscher's images are logical parameters that sustain an impression of continuity, never isolating function from practice, compelling us to focus on the user's situations.

VII. Knud Holscher represents humanity in architecture. Hesitating to call him a humanistic architect derives from the fear of wrongfully associating him with a philosophical theory about humanity and the world and dissociating him from his practice as an architect. This hesitation is due not least to the bifurcation between theory and practice, which has created so many contradictions between civilization's needs and the designs with which it seeks to realize them. Humanistic architecture thus leads to pictorialization or idealization of an idea about humanism in general. The architecture subsequently follows suit.

And yet it is easier to see Holscher as relating to anything but idealization, easier to view him as someone who is unceasingly conscious of the concrete nature of people's lives. He is aware that people's lives unfold physically, bodily. It is precisely this that is the true challenge to space and objects, in other words to architecture and design.

Part 2

Universities

In 1967, Knud Holscher introduced structuralism to Danish architecture with his project for the University of Odense. The strong economic growth that took place in Western Europe during the 1950s and 60s resulted in an explosive development in all educational sectors. This created a need for the renovation and expansion of both educational systems and educational facilities. In many countries, competitions were organized regarding the design of universities. One project from the beginning of the 1960s – a competition entry for the University of Bochum in Germany, designed by the firm of Candilis, Josic, and Woods – drew special attention. Although the project received only third prize, its structuralistic ideas came to exert an influence on the development of ideas in other countries, including Denmark. A world of growth and rapid change created a demand for a dynamic objective to address the planning of cities and buildings. They were to be designed as structures that would be open to both growth and adaptation in response to changing usage.

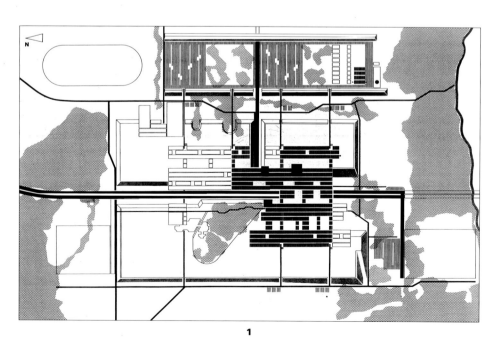

1. First-prize project for the University of Odense, Denmark, 1967. A structuralist plan with multitudinous possibilities for expansion.
2. University of Odense. Detail of the finished building.

The University of Odense, competition proposal

The programm for the new University of Odense was prepared by Denmark's Ministry of Education. It provided that the university would accommodate other, non-traditional and hybrid forms of higher education, and that the expansion would extend over several years.

The university is situated in an open landscape just outside Odense. For the competition proposal, the plan was designed in accordance to a modular grid. This creates a directional structure with possibilities for expansion perpendicular to the approach road that is carried

1, 2. *The buildings are constructed in accordance with a system using dimensionally co-ordinated, prefabricated, concrete, CorTen steel, and glass components. The university is currently still under expansion.*

under the complex of buildings. Small wooded areas characterize the university's landscape. Knud Holscher suggested that they be integrated into the plan's structure and in doing so, created an organic, conditioned form of growth that broke the obvious risk of a uniform structure.

New faculties obtain space by permitting the structure to grow along the central, covered promenade, while growth of the individual faculties occurs with extensions away from the central spine. In harmony with structuralism's philosophy of growth, Knud Holscher avoided introducing monumental elements, for example by not accentuating the main entry. An overriding, architectonic intention regarding the design of the structure's individual elements was that the university, in all phases of expansion, should preserve its comprehensive architectonic identity. This, thereby, strengthens the identity that a centre would otherwise acquire.

The spaces are designed as multi-use spaces, constructed of prefabricated, standardized, interchangeable components. Their expression and distinctive character are generated by their functional contents. In reality, this project is just as much an industrial design project, as it is a traditional building commission. It was, in actuality, the beginning of a professional evolvement that made industrial design one of Knud Holscher's preferred areas of work.

3

4

5

3–5. *The university is situated amidst verdant surroundings. The concrete elements with their polished stone finish, and the rusted-red steel components merge harmoniously with the colours of the rustic landscape.*

The University of Uleåborg, competition proposal

Participation in two design competitions in Finland provided Knud Holscher with yet another possibility for development using structuralism as a strategic planning principle. In 1968, his design of a university in Uleåborg was awarded third prize, and in 1970, his project for Jyväskylä received second prize.

The project for Uleåborg is smilar to the plan for the University of Odense. Here, following the competition brief, it was intended to create a non-authoritarian system, free of symbols. The existing landscaping is also integrated into the plan. Landscape architect, Jørgen Vesterholt's design seeks to preserve the existing wooded areas as much as possible. Like in the University of Odense, the central promenade's function is accentuated as a chain of common areas.

Uleåborg is located north of the Polar Circle. In consideration of the sun's low altitude, tall buildings are avoided. Parking and certain traffic ways are placed below the buildings for climatic reasons.

1. *Competition project for the University of Uleåborg, Finland, 1968.*
2–5. *The central, covered promenade with its chain of common areas functions as the spine of the entire campus. Under expansion, the spine can be extended in harmony with the existing vegetation and terrain.*

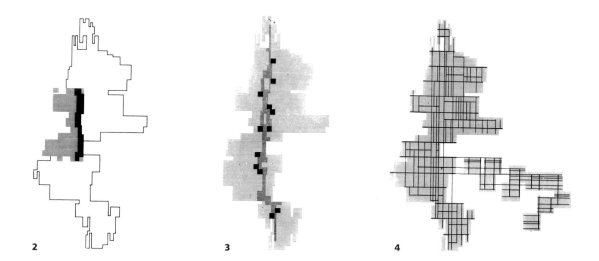

2   3   4

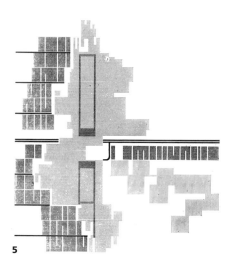

5

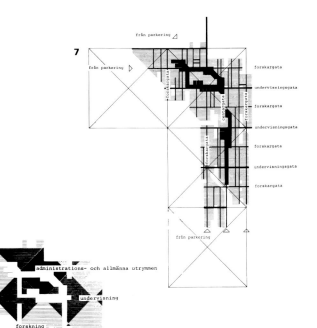

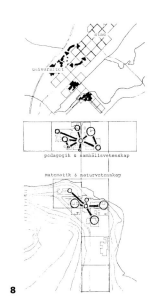

6. *Competition project for the University of Jyväskylä, Finland, 1970. Here, the proximity to the city was decisive in determining the size of the plan's module, as well as the overall organizational structure. The dark areas depict educational functions, while the light areas indicate research areas. This clear functional division demonstrates a series of innovative advantages in relation to the geographic distributions.*

7. *Central, covered promenade and pedestrian circulation system.*

8. *The existing network of Jyväskylä's city structure was also influential to the configuration of the University's expansion.*

9, 10. *Model photos.*

The University of Jyväskylä, competition proposal

The project for the expansion of the existing university in Jyväskylä is designed in response to both the scenic surroundings and the nearby city structure. The plan is organized on a 50 x 50-metre module, which stems from the grid dimensions of the city blocks. The crossing main entries – the diagonals in the modules – facilitate passage and interaction between the research and teaching departments. These features offer the possibility for expansion at different rates without a loss of harmony.

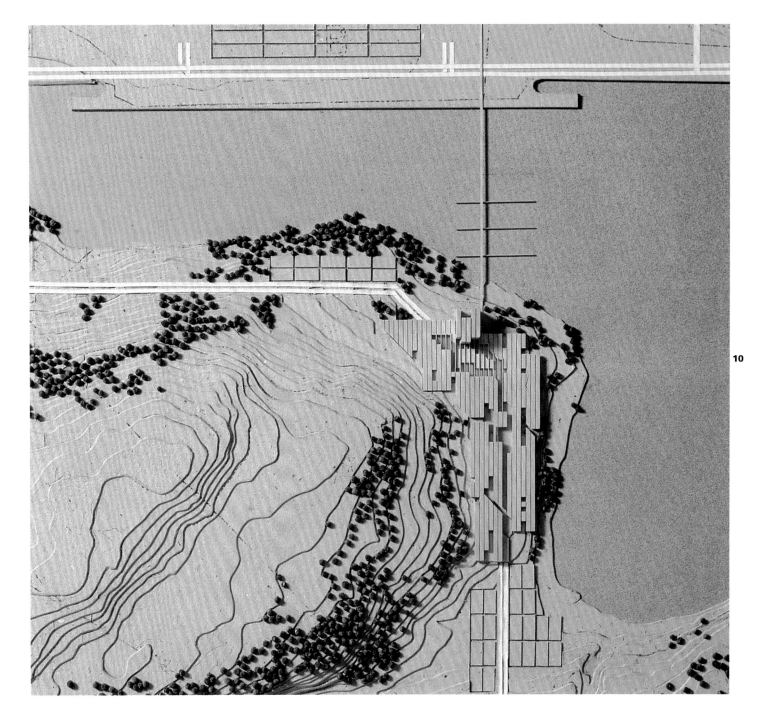

The University of Odense, completed project

The realized project is a modified version of the competition submission. The proposal for underground automobile parking has been abandoned, as with other changes. It was also decided that instead of a prefabricated concrete construction, the buildings should be erected of cast-in-place concrete; an open, column-beam-slab construction with curtain-wall façades. Some of the individual sections of the buildings, such as the auditoriums, are built of concrete as fixed points in the overall, flexible structure.

The complex of buildings erected has a dense building structure, which consists primarily of two-storey buildings with façades of self-supporting, curtain-wall components. The façades are prefabricated; a steel framework upon which glass, sunscreens, and Cor-Ten-coated closure elements are fixed. When the occasion arises, façade components can be taken off and reused in other locations.

The design of the façade components is based on the requirements of weather resistancy, patination, aesthetics, and suitability for production. The façades' detailing, the expression of the components' individual elements, is an essential part of the overall architectonic expression. It gives the complex of buildings their identity and allows the university to be seen as a unified whole at every level of expansion.

Cor-Ten steel is used for the façade components instead of painted or coated panels because it becomes more beautiful as it weathers and patinas over time. The rusted-red colour is natural to the material, which like brick integrates the buildings in a harmonic relationship with the surrounding landscape.

Cor-Ten steel had first demonstrated its weather resistancy in the USA. However, in the humid Danish climate, problems with corrosion arose and in one of the expansion stages, lightly-lacquered, aluminum panels were used as substitutes for the Cor-Ten steel. This substitution revealed that Cor-Ten steel is, aesthetically, the superior material and should be used again in future expansions. The problems of corrosion have now been prevented.

2–4. Both the walls and ceilings of the promenade have been executed in smooth-finished concrete. Other portions of the building are of Cor-Ten steel. The interiors are enriched by the introduction of vegetation, as well as large windows that open out towards the fertile surroundings.

1. A double-height foyer space located along the central promenade.

With the occupation of the first phase of building in 1973, the university consisted of the faculties for medicine, anatomy, and chemistry. Later, the various humanities and several other faculties were added. This required special arrangement of the many spaces that were varied in size but otherwise of the same simple, basic form. As a result, certain spaces became two stories in height.

The interior walkways connect the various building sections. The common areas, auditoriums, library, and cafeteria, are all strategically located adjacent to the central promenade. They are grouped together in close proximity, which makes it possible for the double-storey spaces to receive natural, overhead lighting.

1

2

1–3. The architectonic unity of the project has been preserved over the course of an extensive period of development by always using the same system of façade components. Monotony is avoided by varying the component combinations in accordance to the different demands of each new phase of building.

3

4. *The flexibility of this structuralist approach is also used in the design of the individual buildings. This concept makes it possible to readily change and supplement the network of building services, which supply the educational facilities and laboratories.*

The unique layout of the common areas and the use of plants and graphic art counteract the systemization and standardization, achieving a varied environment and a central promenade that is always populated. The shifting views to the various courtyard gardens and the park-like surroundings offer impressions of fecundity.

The interiors are characterized by the use of robust materials. Concrete walls have a smooth finish, but are otherwise untreated. The floors in the corridors are concrete pavers and the suspended ceilings are rusted, steel grilles. The screens around the cloakrooms and cafeteria furnishings are orange-yellow in colour. The furnishings in the auditoriums are also in pronounced colours. Many of the departments require their own laboratories and auditoriums with advanced equipment. This system of building makes it easy both to provide and access supply lines for the changing and supplementation of such installations.

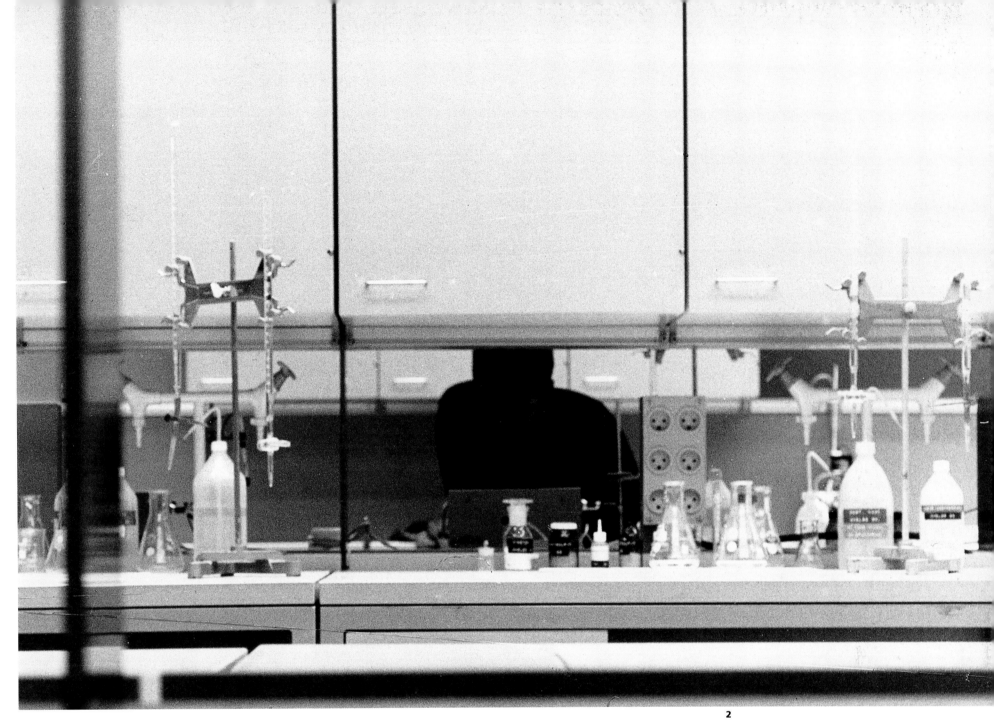

2

po furniture system

The white walls and large windows in the laboratories create a neutral frame for the many, varied activities that take place. The colourful furnishings and the numerous equipment combinations provide the laboratories with their life and distinctive character.

A system of functional furnishings with fixed, installation support stands and working platforms was developed for the laboratories so that loose fixtures can be integrated with ease. Each laboratory is equipped with functionally flexible tables, shelves, cabinets, and other such elements, which were developed in consideration with the laboratories' changing functions. It is an adaptable system, which allows for limitless different layouts in response to the diverse experiments of the laboratories. The stands are simply constructed of steel, while the cabinets and shelving units are built to cabinetmaker quality.

The system is manufactured under the name po system and is used extensively by other architects in the design of public buildings and private research facilities.

1, 2. The laboratory furnishings at the University of Odense are based upon a system of calibrated, uniform modulars, which allow for effortless modifications and renovations in response to the constantly changing demands of the ongoing research.

1

Knud Holscher's own house, Holte

An architect's own house can be considered a manifest, a statement about attitudes, temperaments, and ideals. Every building and design commission must satisfy a series of often incompatible demands. Economy, function, technology, and aesthetics must be reciprocally balanced in the final design. The analysis lies in the preliminary sketches; the synthesis is the architecture.

A building site's distinctive character and prospective, scenic qualities can be very determinative, and just as with the University of Odense, the design evolved from the site's topography. Constructed on a site in a residential neighbourhood, Knud Holscher's own house

2

is designed so that it closes towards the neighbouring properties but opens towards the defining garden spaces. The sloping terrain influences both the house's plan and section, regulating the structure into two horizontal terraces.

The house is designed for use by a family with children and is spacious and light. The main wing contains the parent's private space, as well as a place for social gatherings with family and friends. The children's rooms and a guestroom are situated in a side wing, around a common space illuminated by natural, overhead light. A part of the main wing's living room is two stories in height and has a window spanning the entire east-oriented wall. The bathrooms on both floors are housed in a centrally located installation-core.

1. *Evening picture.*
2. *Detail of the water garden.*
3. *Plan and Section.*
5. *House and water garden.*

3

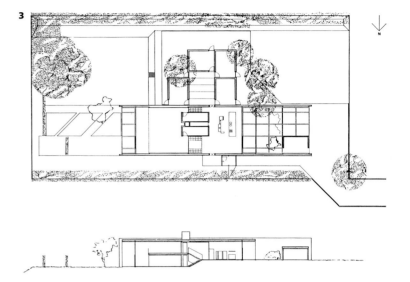

4

Great emphasis was placed on creating a functionally efficient plan in an ordered manner that would not limit the family's possibilities for both collective and individual activities. At the same time, the overall form expresses a minimalism commensurate with the architectural ideals of Mies van der Rohe.

The house is constructed of two parallel, brown brick walls upon which precast concrete deck and roof components are placed. The brick work is untreated both internally and externally. The ceilings are simply the smooth undersides of the concrete components. The floors are covered with white ceramic tiles. The end walls of the main wing are predominately glass set in slender, steel profiles. The side wing is constructed of brick.

Minimalism also characterizes the detailing and furnishings throughout the house, which include furniture designed by Poul Kjærholm. This minimalism, however, does not prohibit a richness of expressions and atmospheres. On the contrary, the dialogue between the house and the garden is open to the constantly changing views of the seasons and the days' shifting light. The boundary between interior and exterior is transient as in traditional Japanese architecture.

The balance between the numerous considerations that enter into the decision-making process imply an infinite range of possibilities. Final choices are made based on an aesthetic consideration of the whole, into which irrational elements of an artistic nature may be included. It is talent which determines if the final result is beautiful and inspiring – as in this house.

2

1. *View from the living-room.*
2, 4. *Kitchen seen from courtyard.*
3. *Interior.*

3

1

4

Calle del Traghetto   Venedig   april 1980   hm.

Part 3

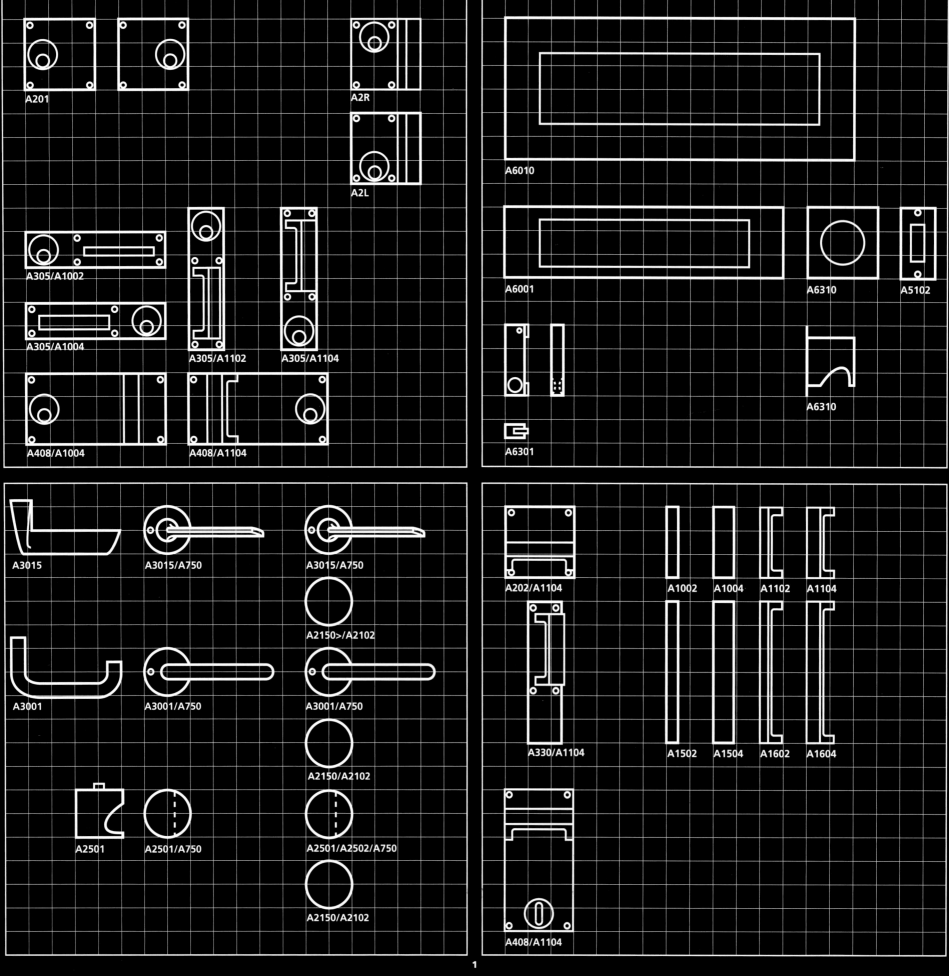

A201

A2R

A2L

A305/A1002

A305/A1004

A305/A1102

A305/A1104

A408/A1004

A408/A1104

A6010

A6001

A6310

A5102

A6310

A6301

A3015

A3015/A750

A3015/A750

A2150>/A2102

A3001

A3001/A750

A3001/A750

A2150/A2102

A2501

A2501/A750

A2501/A2502/A750

A2150/A2102

A202/A1104

A1002 A1004 A1102 A1104

A330/A1104

A1502 A1504 A1602 A1604

A408/A1104

1

Allgood Modric

During the 1960s, it was always a complicated task for architects to select building fittings for major building commissions. The fittings available during that time were produced by several different manufactures and were often characterized by completely different design ideals.

From 1964 to 1966, Knud Holscher was the project architect for the building of St. Catherine's College in Oxford designed by Arne Jacobsen. Together with the English industrial designer, Alan Tye, Holscher developed a series of building fittings, which fulfilled the majority of this building's needs. The series was entitled Modric and was sold and manufactured by G & S Allgood Ltd. It was the first comprehensively designed fitting series ever created. Moreover, it was innovative because it was designed based on the metric system at a time when the metric system had just been newly introduced in Great Britain.

Modric is fabricated in aluminum with the majority of its parts able to be cut from rolled aluminium plates. The other parts of the series are produced by either casting or extrusion. In order to ease scale co-ordinations, a small number of components are able to be combined to create several, different fitting forms.

Industrial design must simultaneously satisfy different functional, technological, and economical demands. The design of a fitting must appeal to those both using and designing buildings. A fitting design must, therefore, be simple and applicable to several, diverse situations. Extensive distribution proves that Modric possesses such attributes. Designers, world wide, support themselves with Modric's catalogue series;

1, 2. *Modric is based on a few very basic forms, which are combined to create numerous variations.*
3. *Door handle and keyhole.*
4. *Door handles.*

a series whose informative systemization and distinguished graphic design have acquired many imitators over the years. Modric has received several honours, amongst others The English Design Award.

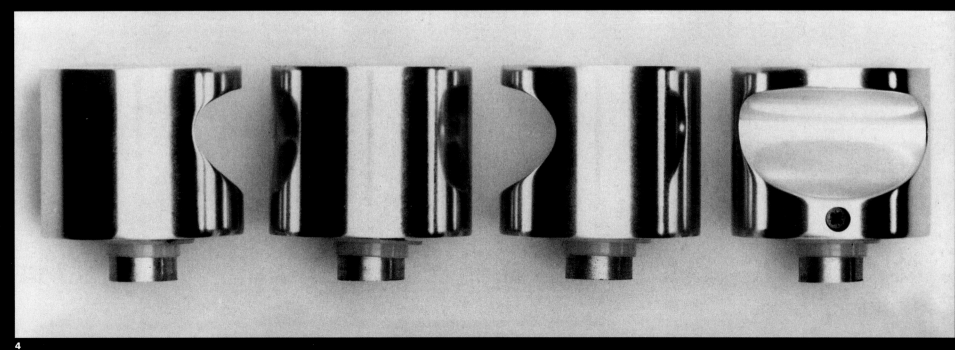

mary expression.

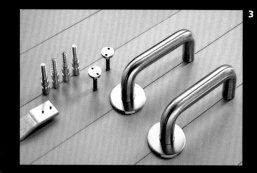

3

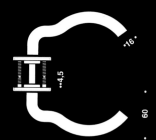

·16·

··4,5

·60·

4

5

This design concept made it possible to combine a relatively small number of components to create a diversity of different fittings. The fittings are suitable for use in most architectural environs, including domestic, institutional, hospital, and industrial buildings. The choice of stainless steel and the simple, robust forms make the fittings usable under the most vulnerable of situations, for example on offshore drilling complexes.

The basic geometric and interrelated forms are to the advantage of the manufacturing process, but also serve to create order and continuity in a diversity of spaces. d line is the world's most extensive and comprehensive range of stainless steel fittings. It includes over 400 products and over 3000 catalogued combinations and is used by the world's leading architects. The series' timeless form and high-quality aesthetics make it possible for a continuously expanding distribution of the fittings – even today, more than twenty years after the introduction of the series.

6

7

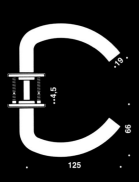

·19·

··4,5

66

125

· 38 ·

50

··3

··4,5

·14·

75
105

32

125
143

8

1. Door handle.
2. Drawer handle.
3. Door handles and related components.
4, 5. Door handles for commercial use.
6. Bathroom shelf.
7. Numerals and letters.
8. Paper-towel dispenser.

A comprehensive graphic design consisting of user instructions, product brochure, and main catalogue was designed based on a system, which accounts for installation dimensions and possibilities for use. The series' graphic design was granted the Danish IG Award for its wide accessibility and high-quality aesthetics. The d line series itself has received the ID Prize, the German Rote Punkt Award, as well as the IF Award.

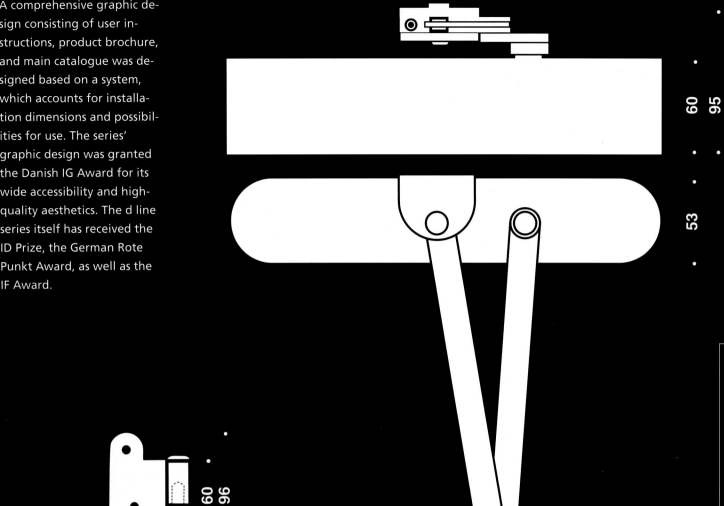

60 95

53

60 96

22

45

292

d line
Lever handles   A

d line lever handle range is offered in two diameters, 16 mm and 19 mm and in six shapes: straight(2), safety(2), cranked and cranked offset, with lever handle accessories on either roses or backplates.

Roses – either concealed with snap-on covers or solid with visible fixings.

Specification Examples.
Lever handles on ball bearing roses.
Lever handles, stainless steel, 16 mm safety with ball bearing roses and lever key escutcheons, door thickness 40 mm, is specified as follows.
1 pair handles with roses
14.1216.02.017
2 pcs. lever key escutcheons
14.3235.02.004
2 pcs. back to back fixing bolts
14.2961.74.077

Backplates – solid with visible fixings positioned to meet the technical needs of individual lock manufacturers (see code index page H101.0 and H102.0).

Ball bearing (patented) – a ring of steel balls in a shallow cup surrounds the neck of the lever handle, using a unique fixing method giving minimal insert projection and wear.

Tests performed by the independent Danish test institute Force Instituttet and various English test institutes have proven d line's superior strength and resulted in a PSA MOB approval (severe duty) – a result of many years product development.

or
Lever handles, stainless steel, 19 mm staight with square backplates with ball bearing, suitable for euro cylinder, door thickness 55 mm, is specified as follows.

2 half set handles 14.1610.02.906
1 pc backplate
14.3875.02 KO: right hand
1 pc backplate
14.3875.02 KO: left hand
4 pcs back to back fixing bolts
14.2961.74.077

Knud Holscher Industriel Design   Produced in Denmark by d line® international as

d line   A119.0

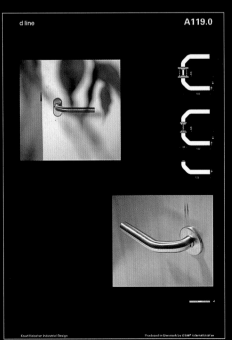

Knud Holscher Industriel Design   Produced in Denmark by d line® international as

d line   A114.0

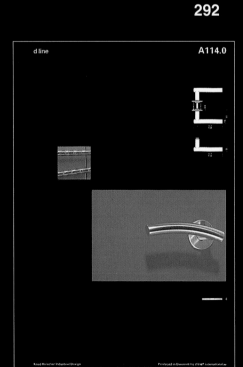

Knud Holscher Industriel Design   Produced in Denmark by d line® international as

d line   A104.1

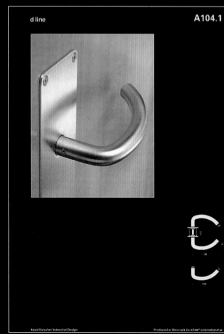

Knud Holscher Industriel Design   Produced in Denmark by d line® international as

d line   A133.0

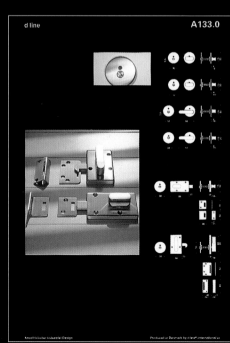

Knud Holscher Industriel Design   Produced in Denmark by d line® international as

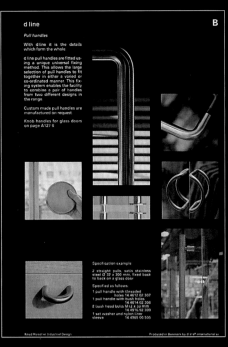

d line

B

Pull handles

With d line it is the details which form the whole

d line pull handles are fitted using a unique universal fixing method. This allows the large selection of pull handles to fit together in either a varied or co-ordinated manner. This fixing system enables the facility to combine a pair of handles from two different designs in the range

Custom made pull handles are manufactured on request

Knob handles for glass doors on page A127.0

Specification example

2 straight pulls, satin stainless steel Ø 32 x 300 mm, fixed back to back on a glass door

Specified as follows
1 pull handle with threaded holes 14.4612.02.307
1 pull handle with bush holes 14.4614.02.306
2 bush head bolts M12 x 30 mm 14.4915.92.309
1 set washer and nylon liner sleeve 14.4965.00.505

Knud Holscher Industrial Design   Produced in Denmark by d line® international as

---

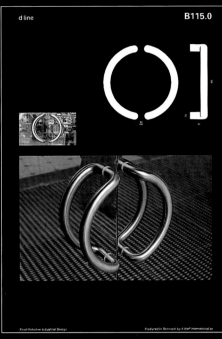

d line

B115.0

Knud Holscher Industrial Design   Produced in Denmark by d line® international as

---

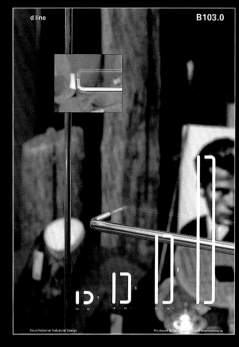

d line

B103.0

Knud Holscher Industrial Design   Produced in Denmark by d line® international as

---

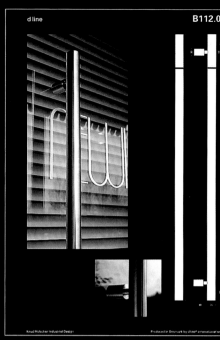

d line

B112.0

Knud Holscher Industrial Design   Produced in Denmark by d line® international as

---

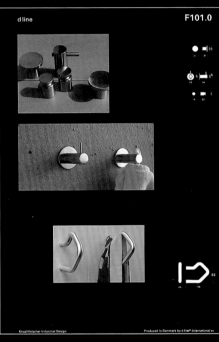

d line

F101.0

Knud Holscher Industrial Design   Produced in Denmark by d line® international as

---

d line

F103.0

Knud Holscher Industrial Design   Produced in Denmark by d line® international as

---

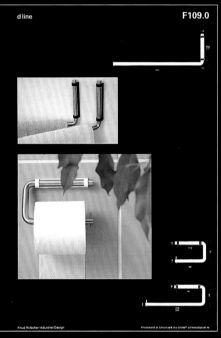

d line

F109.0

Knud Holscher Industrial Design   Produced in Denmark by d line® international as

---

The d line catalogue is designed and systematized so that it contains all the necessary information needed by those planning buildings, and so that all of the fitting details may be easily referenced.

d line

F111.1

Knud Holscher Industrial Design   Produced in Denmark by d line® international as

---

d line

F112.0

Knud Holscher Industrial Design   Produced in Denmark by d line® international as

---

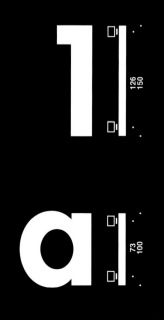

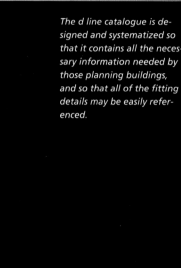

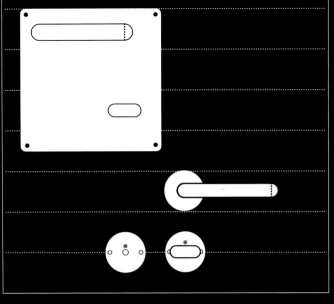

d line is distributed by agents in approximately 40 countries throughout the world. For the purpose of marketing d line, Knud Holscher developed a system of modular panels for use in temporary and permanent exhibitions. They can be assembled and disassembled with the use of standard hand tools.

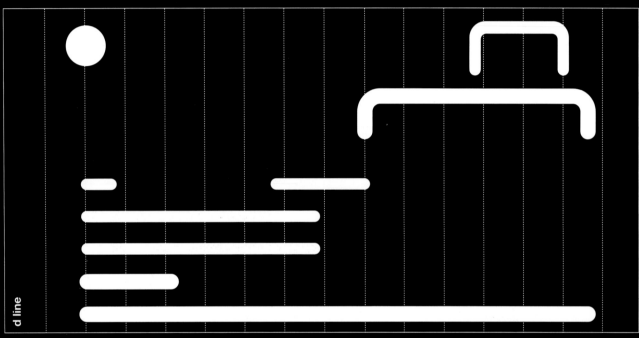

d line

d line

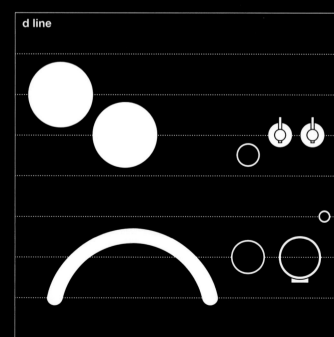

1

2

3

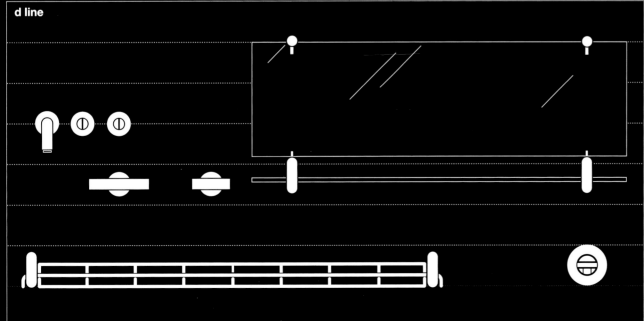

d line

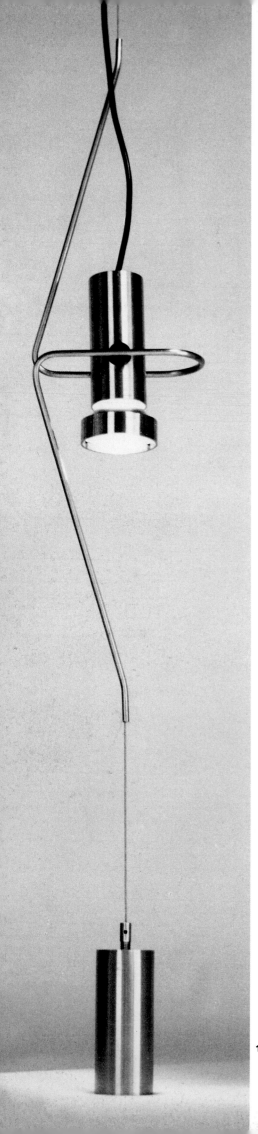

Stringline

The Stringline lamp series
was developed for the firm,
H. F. Belysning. Like so many
of Knud Holscher's other projects, it had the objective of
creating a large number of
variations by combining a
few, individually produced
components. In each combination, the same spot bulb
and conical steel shade are
used to provide optimal visual comfort and minimize the
effects of glare. A fastening
clamp and a few different
support structures can be
combined to form 14 different lamp models.

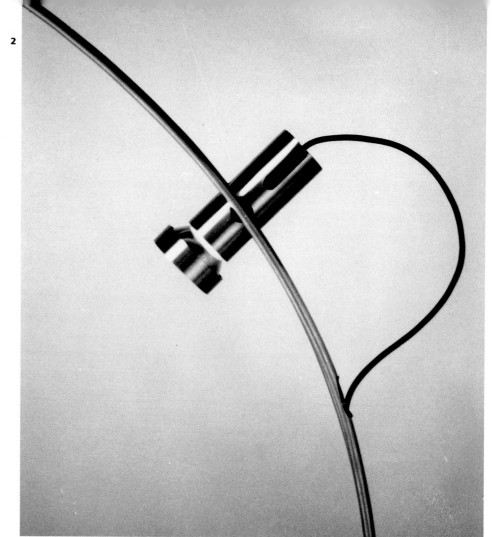

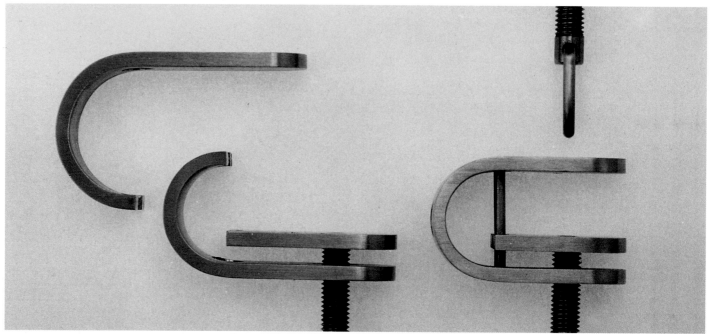

1

3

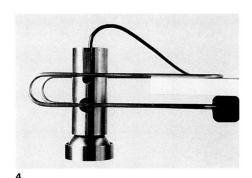

4

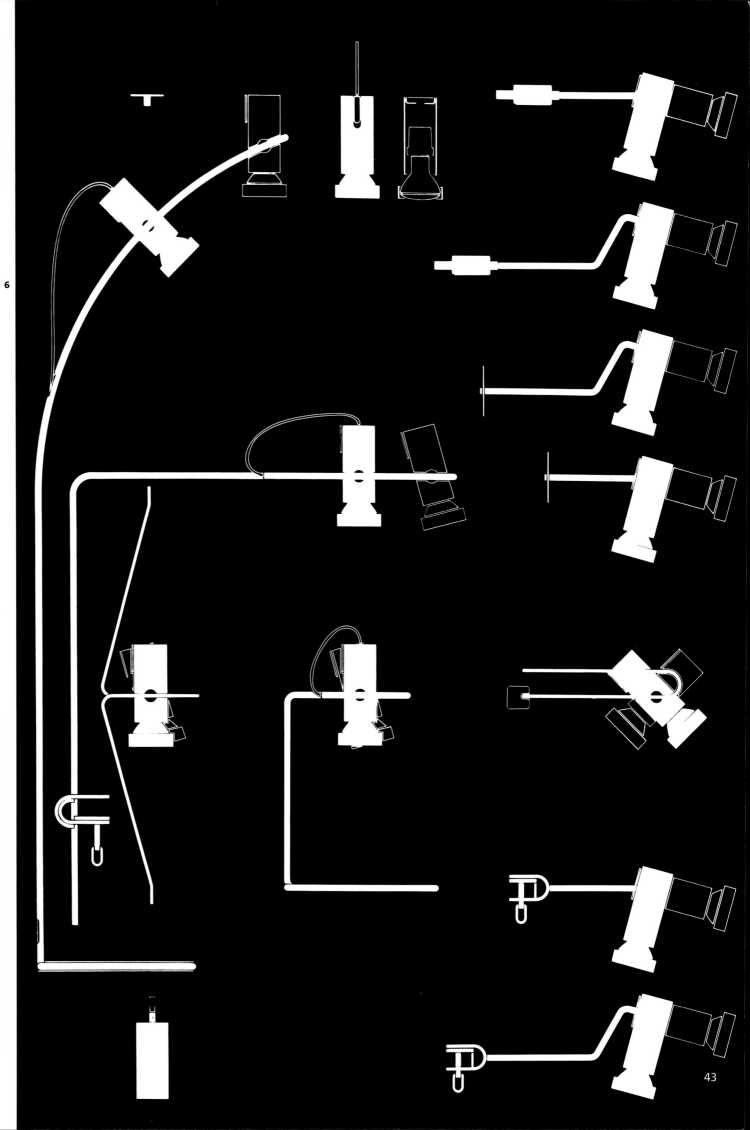

6

1. *A free-hanging weight pulls the suspension wire in tension, stabilizing the lamp in the desired position.*
2. *The reading lamp has a curved support stand, which secures the position of the fixture.*
3. *A fastening clamp is used to attach a steel support arm to the desktop.*
4. *Bookshelf luminary.*
5. *Desktop luminary.*
6. *System drawing.*

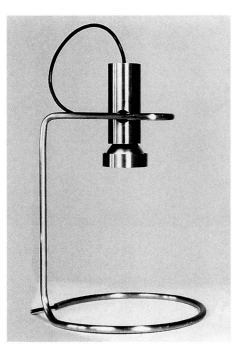

5

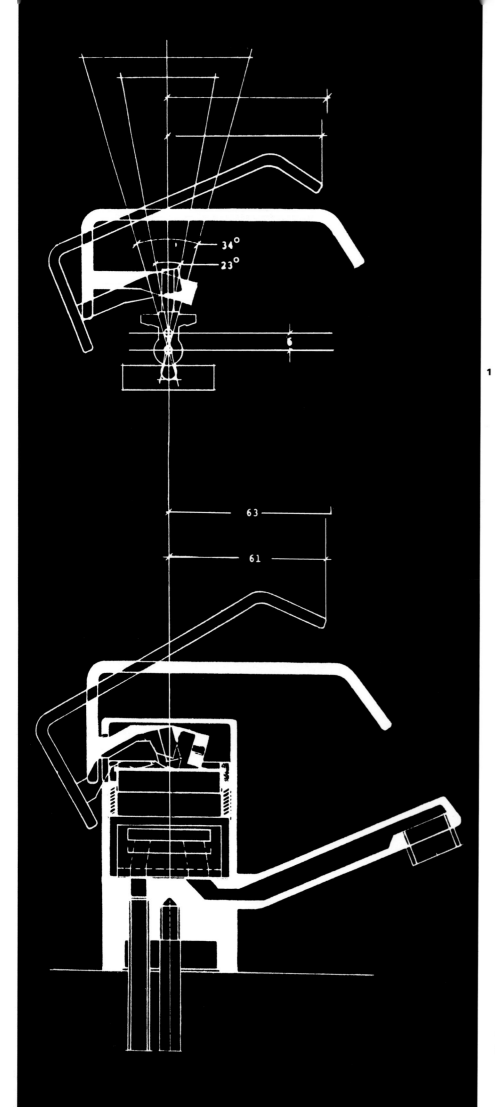

Toni fittings, t line

Denmark is comprised of many, small industrial companies. In order to compete with large, foreign corporations they attempt to develop products that offer superior functional and aesthetic distinction. Industrial design can therefore be of vital importance.

In 1985, Toni Armatur A/S, producer of water faucets for the kitchen and bath, was given the opportunity to use newly developed, German produced, ceramic liners for the design of new water faucets. The inserts were unique because they did not calcify like traditional gaskets. Knud Holscher designed a faucet that conditioned the use of the liners. It became the first fitting with a ceramic, closing device ever produced in Denmark.

The faucet is fabricated in brass and has a robust form that was determined by the need for an easy and immediately comprehensible operation. Both the psychology of perception and ergonomics were taken into consideration so that hospital patients upon first sight, could use the faucet. The faucet is available in either a polished or satin chromium-plated finish or can be enamelled in different colours.

1. *Detail drawing.*
2, 3. *Enamelled faucet.*

3

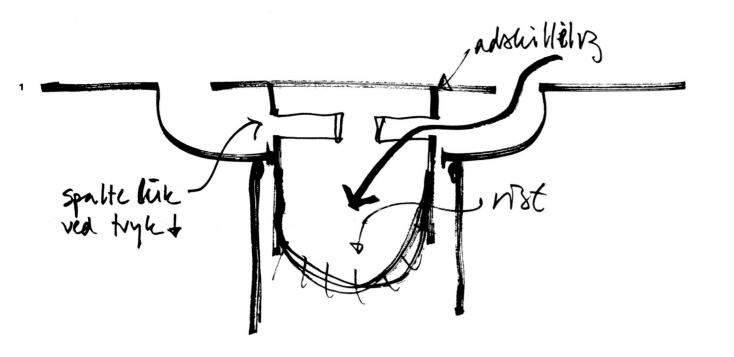

1

adskillelvs

spalte luk ved tryk↓

rist

IFÖ stainless steel sink, Concert

An analysis of the work that typically takes place around a kitchen sink reveals that the work can be eased with a thoughtful design for the sink. The preparing of meats and vegetables, the washing of dishes, and the sorting of rubbish place different requirements on the design. The demands of hygiene and a suitable design for the water and drain connections must also be taken into account.

The Concert stainless steel kitchen, designed by Knud Holscher and produced by IFÖ, is based upon the combination of a few, principal forms. The design spans from

1. *Sketch of the unique drain-screen design that provides a flush surface on the bottom of the sink. This detail is a clear, aesthetic solution to the typical problem of the visually unappealing, dark reveal occurring at the mouth of the drain.*

2. *Double-basin kitchen sink.*
3. *Geometrically formed sink details.*
4. *Kitchen sink complete with cutting board, colander, dish-drying rack, and dish-draining tray.*

2

the very simple work sink to the multifunctional, double-basin sink equipped with place for the sorting of rubbish and a larger area for the preparation of meals. There are 19 combinations in all, including many accessories, such as cutting board, colander, dish-drying rack, and dish-draining tray. The design is of the highest functional and aesthetic resolve.

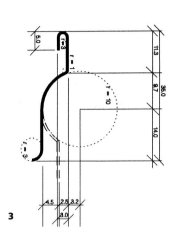

3

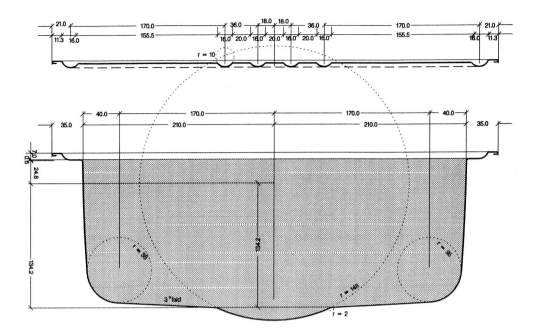

4

1. *Aqua bidet.*
2. *Model photos of preliminary design studies for the competitions.*
3. *Wall hung and floor mounted bidets.*
4. *Pressalit seat for Aqua.*

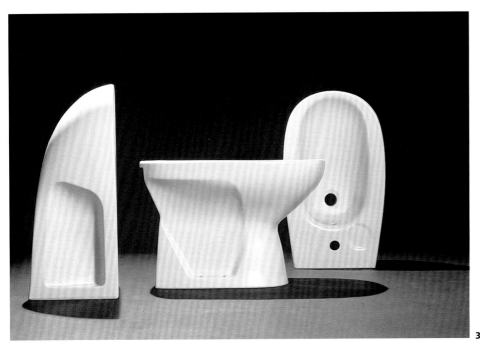

4

3

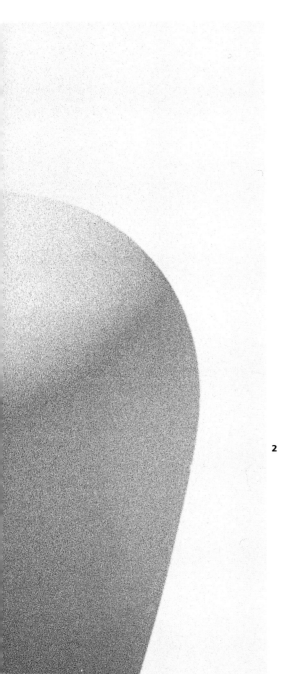

2

IFÖ series, Aqua

The design of lavatories and water closets in sanitary porcelain presents great challenges. The primary objective of the Aqua design was to create a beautiful and harmonic form that simultaneously considered the demands of a complex production process. An effective flushing and emptying placed special demands on the design, while the user required attention to ergonomic and hygienic concerns.

In 1963, together with Alan Tye, Knud Holscher won a competition organized by Ideal Standard for the design of a lavatory, water closet, and bidet. In concert with his English partner he obtained contact with the firm of Adamsez. Adamsez, owned by the Adams brothers, was known for its design-quality, sanitary porcelain; a product especially valued by architects. Working in collaboration with one of the Adams brothers, the necessary modelling work was executed and the Meridian One series was able to be put into production relatively quickly. In 1965, Meridian One was conferred the British Design Award.

In the beginning of the 1970s, following his return to Denmark, Knud Holscher began a collaborative effort with the Swedish firm, IFÖ. The first result of this collaboration was a patentable lavatory based on the design of a special, reverse drain trap. The lavatory has been used extensively in the hospitals of Hvidovre and Herlev municipalities.

Knud Holscher obtained the commission for the design of a new series of bathroom plumbing fixtures after winning an invitational design competition held by IFÖ. Development of the new series Aqua – spanned over eight years. The final design was a great success, owing much to its elegant, sculptural forms.

Following another invitational design competition in 1996, IFÖ, presented yet another new series of bathroom plumbing fixtures designed by Knud Holscher. The series, entitled Ceranova, has received the Swedish Design Award and Stuttgart Design Zentrum's Roter Punkt Award.

1. *First prize project for the new IFÖ Aqua series.*
2. *The Aqua series suited for production.*
3. *Aqua lavatories.*
4. *Hospital lavatory with porcelain drain trap.*

JÖMÖW OKT. 1988 kHoscher

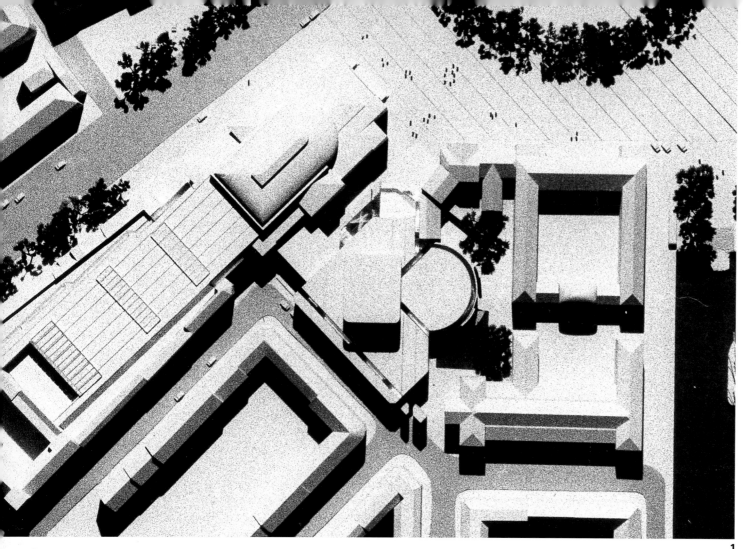

1

Royal Theatre, Copenhagen

The Royal Theatre in Copenhagen is home to the arts of drama, opera, and ballet. Today, only opera and ballet remain in the original theatre building dating from 1874. At the end of the 1920s a theatre for drama was built in connection to the old theater. This theatre, which also functioned initially as a concert hall for the new State Broadcasting Service, proved to be poorly suited for both purposes.

In 1978, after many disappointing plans for the building of a new theatre for drama, the Minister of Cultural Affairs organized a competition for an addition to the original theatre building. Three proposals were selected, each with a characteristically different placement of the building. They were to provide the foundations for the continuously suspended planning that would take place over the next several years.

The preferred proposal was designed by Knud Holscher and Svend Axelsson. It recommended that the theatre building dating from 1931 be demolished and that a new theatre be erected in its place. The new building would be directly connected to the original theatre building, yet would have its own entry from Kongens Nytorv. It was a building which, in the jury's opinion, provided many admirable conditions for the public, the actors, and the stage technicians.

1. Competition proposal for the expansion of the Royal Theatre in Copenhagen.
2–5. Proposal for a stage with possibilities for different arrangements.
6. Model photo showing the main entry from Kongens Nytorv and the square facing Charlottenborg.
7. Conceptual model of the design of the theatre's acoustic ceiling.

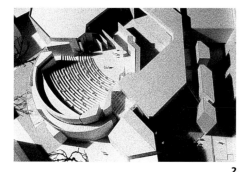

2

4

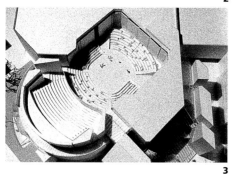

3

5

6

7

The proposal for the theatre was designed so that the stage could be arranged for both traditional and non-traditional theatre performances. The old and the new theatres would thus obtain a common, ancillary stage. The design of the exterior façades respected the existing, neighbouring context of historically preserved buildings.

Following a lengthy delay, the Minister of Cultural Affairs decided that for the first phase the new building should only consist of improvements to the existing theatre, i.e. incorporating improved stage technologies within the theatre from 1931. The commission was divided between Nils Koppel, the architect to date, and the team of Knud Holscher and Svend Axelsson.

1, 2. *The actors' greenroom in the addition to the Royal Theatre.*
3. *View of the new addition facing Holmens Kanal. The structure contains workshops, rehearsal halls and administrative facilities.*

Holscher and Axelsson are responsible for the recently completed rehearsal halls, workshops, and actors' green-rooms. The actors' green-rooms are a five-storey high space, enriched by natural, overhead lighting and comfortable furnishings. The connections between the floor levels of the old and new theatres act as balconies within the space. The frontal surfaces of the balconies are adorned by the work of the visual artist, Svend Wiig Hansen.

The new building, housing workshops and rehearsal halls, is situated between two buildings dating from the previous century. The front façade's band of windows provides a pensive pause in a row of ornate façades. The rear façade neutrally adapts to the existing urban fabric.

3

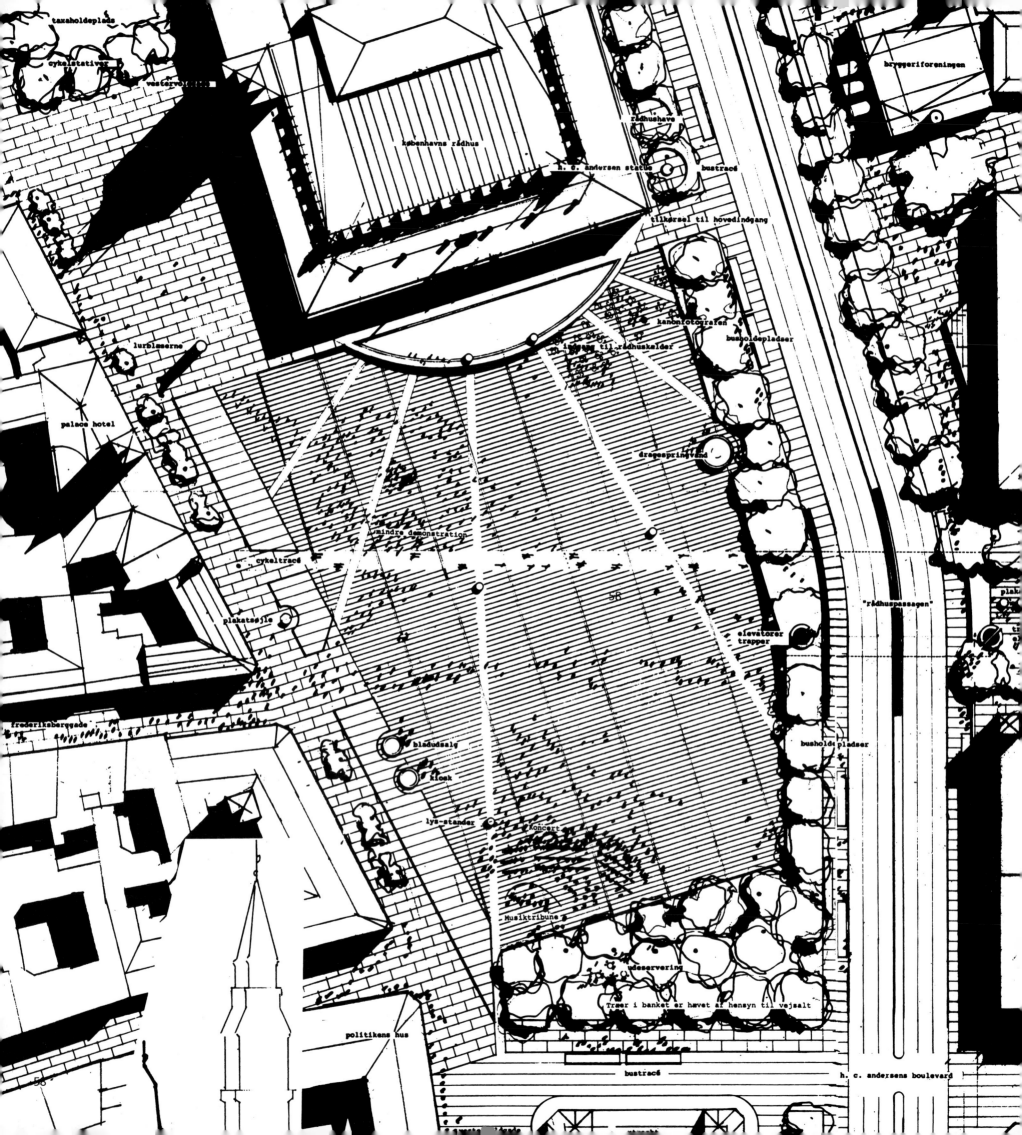

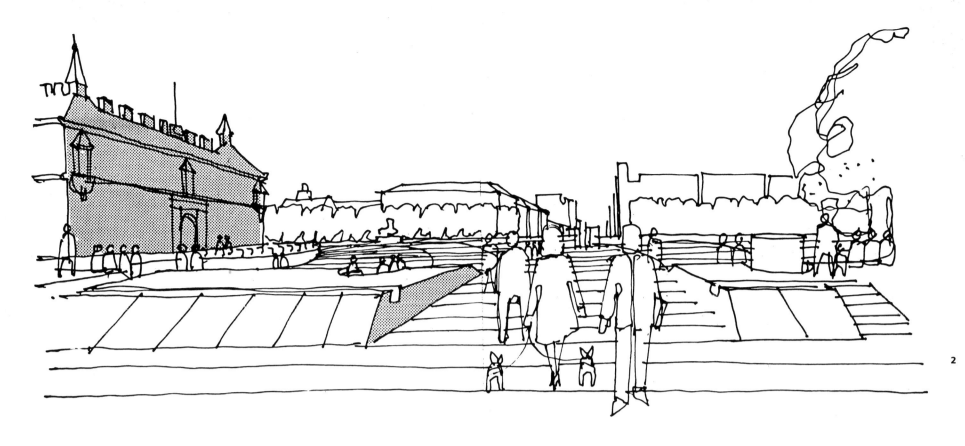

1. *Site plan.*
2. *Sketch.*

Town-Hall Square, Copenhagen

When the square in front of the Copenhagen Town Hall was established at the beginning of this century, its design was closely linked to the recently built town hall. However, with time, this relationship had been weakened by numerous changes carried out to the square. The square's boundaries were already less than clear, and it was further divided by a very busy street.

Over the course of several years, various competitions have been devised calling for a new design for the square. The most recent competition dates from 1979, and was won by Knud Holscher and Svend Axelsson.

They suggest removing the very busy street that cuts the square in two. They also recommend that the street running between the square and the historic city centre be rerouted. By providing the square with a shell form, slightly sloping towards the town hall, some of the lost ties to the town hall could be re-established.

The town hall often forms a backdrop to festive events, drawing large crowds to the square. Defining the square's boundaries, for example, with rows of trees would further strengthen the character of this urban space. Removing the through-going traffic from the street along the square's eastside would create direct access to the inner city's chain of pedestrian streets.

Some of the main features of Holscher and Axelsson's plan were realized in 1996 with a renovation of the Town Hall Square.

2

Jægersborg Centre, Copenhagen

Jægersborg Allé is located north of Copenhagen in the municipality of Gentofte. It is a shopping street with a mixture of both tall and low buildings, dating from various periods. Until the middle of the 1980s an industrial complex, a dairy, existed on the site. Its demolition created space for a new residential development.

A major objective for the design of the new buildings was to preserve the existing, colourful urban fabric. Therefore, the four-storey high building is set back from the street, while the low buildings accommodating retail functions are situated with interstitial spaces that serve to break up the uniformity of the street. The four-storey building houses offices on the lower floors and apartments on the two uppermost floors. The low buildings along the main street are visually appropriate to the many fine examples of 1930s International Modernism that exist in Gentofte.

The residential development at the rear of the site is three storeys in hight with yellow brick facades. Altogether, there are 101 apartments of varying sizes. The largest of these are 94 sqm and are designed with spacious roof terraces. Common to all dwellings are well-designed entrance lobbies, large, light stairwells with elevators, and well-equipped kitchens and bathrooms.

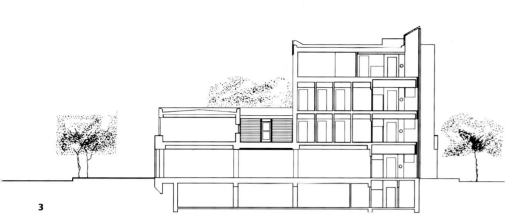

3

4

5

1. *Housing façade.*
2. *Model.*
3. *Section.*
4. *Shopping area.*
5. *Entry to flats.*

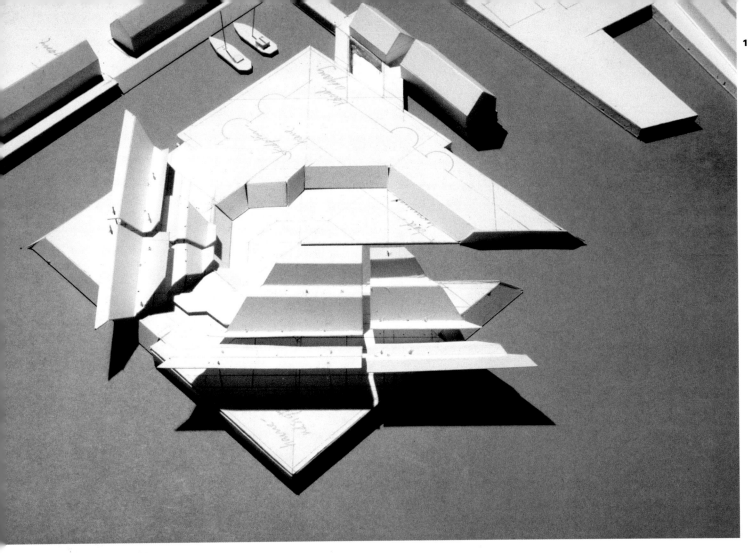

1. Conceptual model for a museum of modern art to be sited in the central area of Copenhagen's old harbour.
2. Site plan.
3. Section through the museum.
4. Sketch.

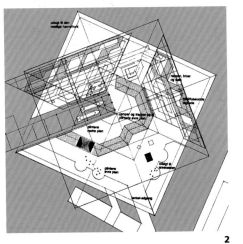

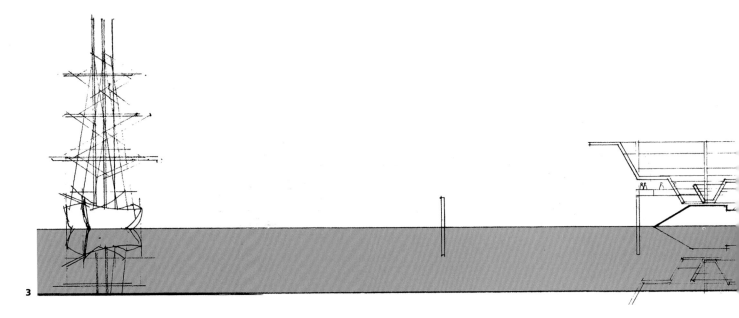

Copenhagen's harbour, proposal

As in other large harbour cities, the dockside functions of Copenhagen's harbour have moved from being, centrally located to being "out of town", where there is more space for the loading and unloading of massive freight containers and cargo. As a result, there is now space for new functions, such as cultural facilities, in the old central harbour areas.

In 1982, Knud Holscher and Svend Axelsson designed a museum of modern art for a publication proposing possible uses for Copenhagen's vacant harbour areas. The project proposal is sited on Christiansholm, immediately opposite the mouth of Nyhavn's main channel. Considering the building's prominent visibility from the promenade along the old harbour front, the building is sculpturally formed.

The museum forms views to the city's profile of towers and domes and is designed to visually rest on the water. The interplay between building and water provides the building's distinctive character. The water is drawn into the museum via a dock for the boats sailing from the city centre. Large cantilevering roofs capture the light's reflection off the water.

The roof is conceived as translucent, white planes that would filter daylight like the diffused, artificial light directed towards works of art. The sequence of spaces and level changes create unexpected perspectives and spatial variations for an enrichment of the visitor's meander through the museum.

The museum rests like a jewel in the teeming life of the harbour; during the day, reflecting the sun's play in the water, during the night, its own illumination reflecting on the water's tranquil surface. The building is a cultural manifest, not because of its contents alone, but because of its architecture as well.

The project has never managed to come further than the pages of a book.

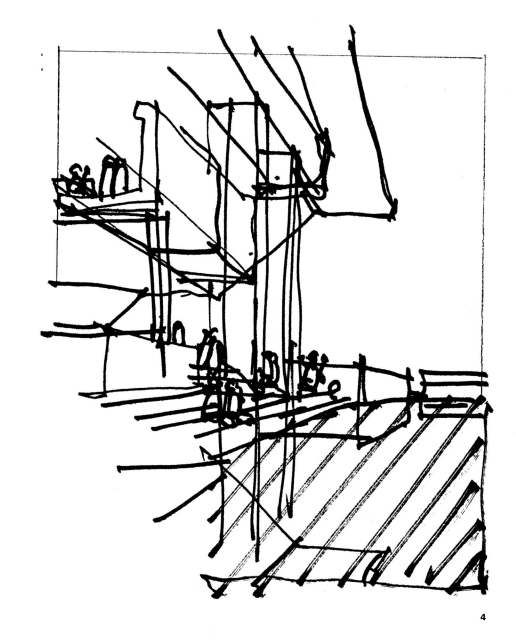

4

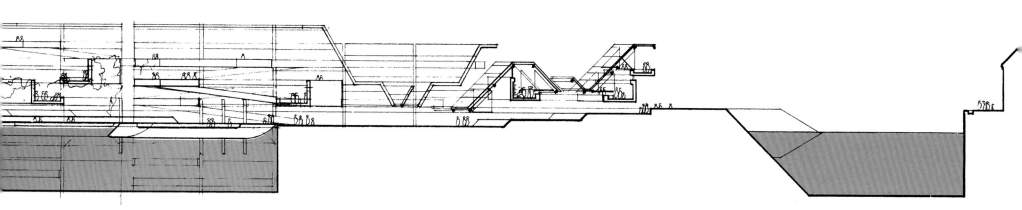

Cultural centre in Neumünster

Neumünster is situated in the German constituent state, Schleswig-Holstein, and has approximately 80,000 inhabitants. In 1979, the city organized an international, invitational design competition for the building of a municipal hall; a cultural centre containing a theatre, concert hall, festival hall, cafe, restaurant, and library. Knud Holscher and Svend Axelsson's project was selected, built, and opened to the public in 1988.

The Neumünster Cultural Centre is sited near a large market place, with a small, park-encircled lake on the opposite side. The restaurant has a large, outdoor terrace oriented towards the lake. The theatre seats 576. Its main stage and ancillary stages are proportioned with space for a complete symphony orchestra, as well as facilities for extensive theatre productions. The festival hall accommodates up to 500 spectators. The double height common foyer has a visually expressive frame construction and is illuminated by natural, overhead lighting. It is clearly the space which attracts the greatest attention.

1

2

3

1. Model of the cultural centre in Neumünster.
2. The foyer serves as a passage for pedestrians moving between the square and the park.
3. Competition sketch.
4. Theatre interior.

4

Swimming centre in Farum

The swimming centre is situated north of Copenhagen in the municipality of Farum. In this residential community of predominately low houses, the building's tall, concrete wall and massive roof plane endow it with a landmark quality. The roof covers the hall's 50-metre long swimming pool, while the changing rooms, clubroom, and cafe are located in the low building that parallels the swim hall.

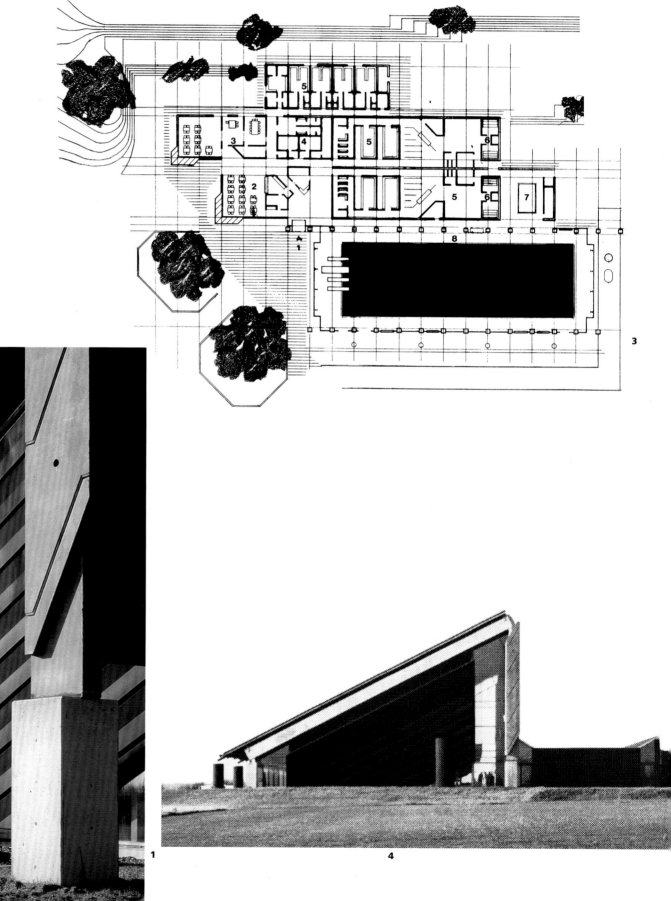

HVOR LANGT KAN DU SE ?
HVIS DU STÅR PÅ STRANDEN
OG SER UD OVER VANDET
KAN DU IKKE SE AFRIKA
ELLER GRØNLAND
ELLER KINA.
MEN DU KAN SE SOLEN
MÅNEN OG STJERNERNE
SOM ER MEGET LÆNGERE BORTE.

DU IKKE KØBE VAND FOR GULD
E HELE LOMMEN FULD.
U PLASKE RUNDT I VAND.
G END JOACHIM VON AND.!

5

6

1. *Gable detail.*
2. *Section.*
3. *Plan.*
4. *The swimming centre rests in the scenic surrounds.*
5. *The walls are decorated with ceramic images created by Bodil and Richard Manz, accompanied by texts from poet, Benny Andersen.*
6. *The building at night.*
7. *Interior.*

7

All aspects of the building have been thoughtfully and rigorously detailed and dimensioned. The concrete surfaces are untreated, while the roof and the solid portions of the end walls are clad in rust-red, Cor-Ten steel panels. The swimming centre stands as a rustic sculpture in the surrounding, verdant landscape.

The building's interior is also rusticated with large concrete beams and a ceiling cladding of wood-fibre-reinforced concrete panels. The end walls of the building are clad in white, Glasal panels. The floors are covered with yellow-brown, ceramic tiles. On the columns, walls, and the bottom of the children's pool are ceramic images designed by Bodil and Richard Manz, with texts by poet, Benny Andersen.

The Copenhagen Airport, Finger B

Copenhagen Airport's International Terminal dates from the end of the 1950s. It has since been expanded in several phases and is currently still under construction. Various architects have been responsible for the different phases of expansion.

The airplanes taxi along three "fingers". The largest of them, Finger B, was designed by Knud Holscher, Svend Axelsson, and Erik Sørensen. Finger B provides direct access to a central area of the terminal building including transit hall, cafes, and shops.

Completed in 1987, Finger B was designed to remedy an older and smaller building. It is constructed of prefabricated, concrete columns and beams, which support a lightweight, steel construction clad in polished, aluminum panels. The interior is clad in thin, fibre-reinforced concrete panels.

The building is two storeys in height. The ground floor accommodates service space and parking for service vehicles. The upper section consists of wide corridors with high ceilings and lounge areas and passenger facilities with drop ceilings. The rounded forms of the building allude to the polished concourse tubes that reach out to the planes – siphoning passengers to and from their desired destinations. The design is an artistic and functional solution that possesses the same technical force as the planes themselves. It is detailed and designed as a piece of industrial design.

The light colours, varying daylight, dampened acoustics, and spaciousness of the interior offer a friendly welcome to passengers coming from the noisy confines of the airplane's cabin.

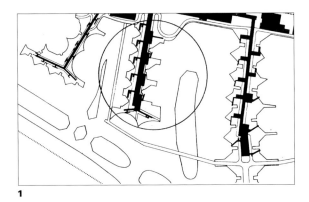

1

2

3

4

1. *Finger B is the central terminal of the airport's three "fingers."*
2. *Façade facing "the apron".*
3. *Fire stair.*
4. *Interior of Finger B.*
5. *Plan and façade.*

5

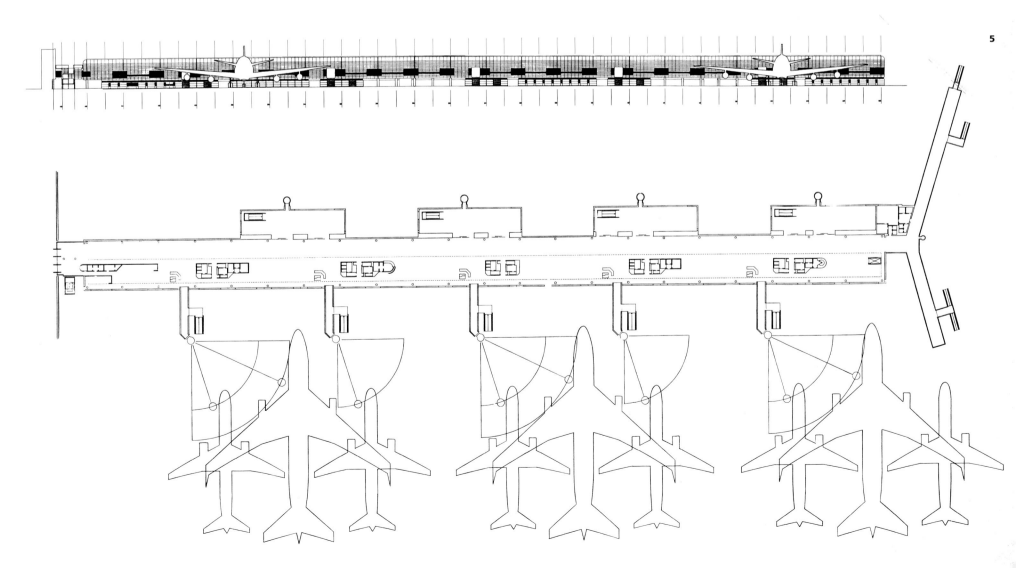

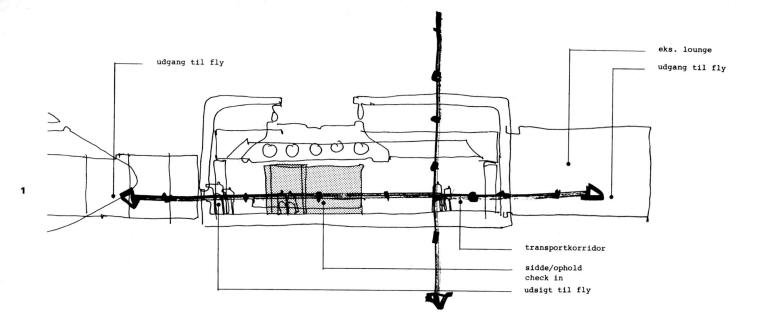

udgang til fly

eks. lounge

udgang til fly

1

transportkorridor

sidde/ophold
check in
udsigt til fly

1–4. Transverse section demonstrating the lighting and ventilation concept for Finger B. On one side of the space is a very busy corridor and on the other, passenger waiting lounges, toilets, and other service facilities.
5, 6. Finger B is designed as a spacious and light passageway.

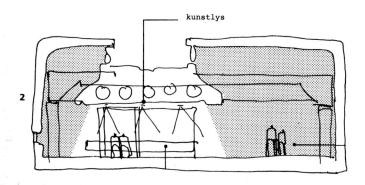

kunstlys

2

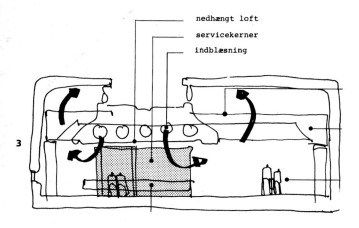

nedhængt loft
servicekerner
indblæsning

3

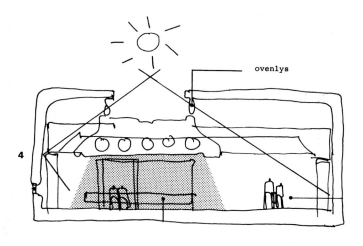

ovenlys

4

A transverse section through Finger B shows that there is full-height over the corridors, while a drop ceiling reduces the height of the lounge areas. The wide row of overhead natural light is diffused and directed towards the periphery walls by means of the drop ceiling. Way-finding signs and other graphic indicators serve to further illuminate the walls. The undersides of the roof beams provide a rhythmic articulation of the long foyer space.

The lounge areas have a seating capacity of 500 and are equipped with their own toilets, telephone booths, and small cafés. In addition, they are located in close proximity to a diversity of services located in the transit hall.

5

6

The Copenhagen Airport, Domestic Terminal

Until 1990, Copenhagen Airport's Domestic Terminal was located in a provisional building. In 1991, the first stage of a new and independent terminal was constructed. It is a long, one-storey building; a high-tech architecture that elegantly harmonizes with the large, shining bodies of the airplanes.

The building façade towards the approach road, an 11-metre tall aluminium screen, serves as a sound barrier against ground noise for the community lying just outside the airport. Towards the taxi and runway area, the building's rounded form and details relate directly to the formal language of the planes. The building is constructed of prefabricated, concrete elements, and lightly plastered masonry work. The exterior of the terminal is covered with aluminium panels.

2

The white walls of the interior are illuminated by diffused, natural lighting stemming from a linear, vaulted skylight running parallel to the walls. Inside the terminal there are seating groups, restaurants, bars, and kiosks. Check-in counters are located near the main entry and baggage reclaim areas close to the exit.

1

3

4

1. Detail of ceiling sky vault and diffuser.
2. Waiting lounge.
3. Terminal building seen from "the apron."
4, 5. The exterior of the terminal is covered with aluminium panels.

5

1

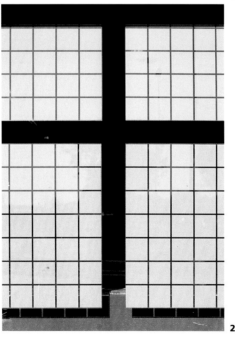

2

3

The Copenhagen Airport, multi-storey car park

The car park located along the approach road to Copenhagen Airport's International Terminal has a definitive architectonic expression that clearly depicts its purpose and function. Despite its size, the structure does not dominate its surroundings. Instead, it relates neutrally to the adjacent terminal building.

Entry and exit ramps are housed in circular towers located at the ends of the car park. The extensive black façades of the towers serve to distinguish them from the reflective glass skin used to clad the rest of the parking structure. The towers visually anchor the car park amidst the airport's network of flowing traffic.

The main façades are of tempered glass plates suspended from the car park's concrete structure. The joint between the glass skin and the concrete frame is both an aesthetically pleasing detail and a functionally efficient solution to ventilation needs. From the exterior, the frosted patterns of the frit glass plates are only faintly discernable against the play of reflections on the surface of the façade. However, the glass patterns become clearly distinguishable once inside the car park's gridded, light-filled interior. At night when the car park is illuminated from within, the structure appears as a glowing and spacious image.

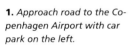

1. *Approach road to the Copenhagen Airport with car park on the left.*
2, 3. *The façades are composed of suspended glass plates. A reveal space between the structure and the glass skin ventilates the parking decks.*
4. *Circulation tower housing the ramps.*
5. *Corner detail.*
6. *Detail of circulation towers housing the ramps.*

Unicon Concrete

In 1986, the large concrete company, Unicon Beton, sponsored a closed competition for the design of its new main office to be located near its production facilities in Roskilde. They invited four architecture firms to compete for the commission. Unicon desired a building with a strong and distinct architectural identity.

Knud Holscher's winning project satisfied this desire. The simple, yet very striking main façade is an easily recognizable symbol seen from the very busy freeway that runs adjacent to the site.

The building is constructed in accordance with a geometrically fixed plan; a two storey, L-shaped building opening onto a central hall with a curved main façade. The L-shaped plan structures a half-square, the diagonal of which forms the main axis of the building. The main entry is located in the interior of the L. The concrete elements employed in the construction of the building are also simple, geometric forms. The white façade components are supported by a steel frame construction and subdivided after a stringent geometric system. The components are fibre reinforced concrete cement sandwich elements with both white and acid washed finishes.

A reflecting pool sited in front of the curved façade, mirrors natural light through the large, screen window, accentuating the double height foyer with a shifting play of light.

The artistic design of the fenestration, the freestanding columns delineating the geometry, and the refined detailing draw much attention. They are testimony that concrete can be commensurate with every other building material if used in the proper design with thoughtful aesthetic consideration. This also, undoubtedly, satisfies the aspirations of the building's proprietor.

1, 2. *The main façade seen from the adjacent-lying freeway advertises Unicon's commitment to quality.*

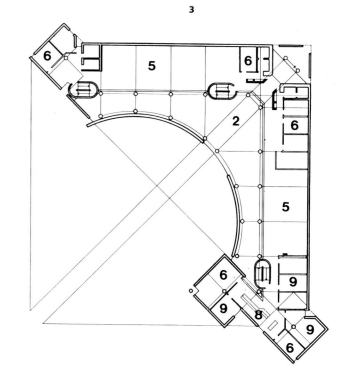

1. main entrance
2. two-storey central hall
3. reception
4. service counter
5. office landscape
6. office/conference room
7. canteen
8. excutive secretaries
9. executive offices

1, 5, 6. *The main foyer provides direct access to the building's offices, as well as space for possible exhibitions.*
2. *Ground floor.*
3. *1st floor.*
4. *Section.*

Dubrovnik 7-Aug. 53 Kolodin

Part 5

1

HT bus shelters

Bus shelters are erected at the majority of bus stop locations in the Copenhagen metropolitan area. Their urban design makes them suitable to all city environments and at the same time clearly indicates the location of a bus stop. Despite the simple form of the glass shelter with a shallow curved roof supported on slender columns, the design is a complex solution to a rigorous set of requirements.

2

The design was developed from Knud Holscher's winning proposal for an invitational design competition sponsored by the Copenhagen Metropolitan Traffic Association. The competition called for the design of a bus stop shelter design that would provide reliable protection against weather and wind, without concealing waiting passengers. It was to be sturdily constructed, easy to maintain, and uninviting to vandals. Finally, it was to be adaptable to a diversity of locations in both dense city environments and open, residential neighbourhoods.

A prototype was constructed and proved to satisfy these requirements. However, it was not until ten years later, and on new terms, that the decision was made to erect the new bus shelters. The manufacturing and distribution of the shelters was open to a competitive, international bid. The bid was won by the Danish-French firm, AFA-JCDecaux, in collaboration with Knud Holscher.

3

1, 3, 4 *The form and function of the bus stop shelter is as simple as that of an umbrella.*
2. *Isometric sketch.*

4

Consequently, the original bid design was modified so that one of the glass walls became an illuminated, advertising display. The bus stop shelter is primarily intended for those standing, however a small bench also allows a pair of passengers to sit while waiting.

In conjunction with the bus stop shelter, a freestanding advertisement screen and a round advertisement pillar were correspondingly designed and erected. Other urban furnishings, for example a cylindrical toilet building, were also created with similar functional and aesthetic articulations.

1

2

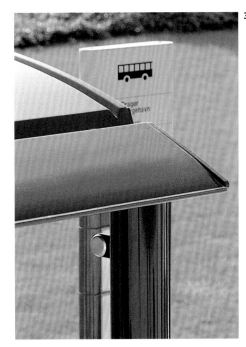

3

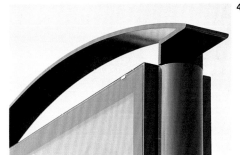

4

5

6

1, 2. *The bus shelters are designed with a glass display wall for the posting of advertisement posters and city maps. During the dark hours of the day the display walls are artificially illuminated.*
3. *Details of the roof.*
4. *Details of the advertisement screen.*
5. *Information column located at a bus stop.*
6. *Freestanding advertisement pillar, which draws its inspiration from the traditional Copenhagen advertisement pillars.*

Georg Jensen, kitchenware

In 1974, the firm of Georg Jensen commissioned Knud Holscher to design a kitchenware set that would be suitable for both indoor and outdoor use. The system of pots, pans, lids, and dishes was produced in cast iron. Cast iron efficiently maintains heat, even when used outdoors. The design accentuates the functional characteristics of the individual pieces. All parts are stackable, requiring minimal cabinet space needed for storage. Cutting boards, wooden dish mats, and stainless steel grilling utensils and cutlery also from part of to the series.

Georg Jensen is no longer a manufacturer of kitchenware products.

1. *Sketch.*
2. *System drawing.*
3–10. *Pots, pans lids, and dishes produced in cast iron.*

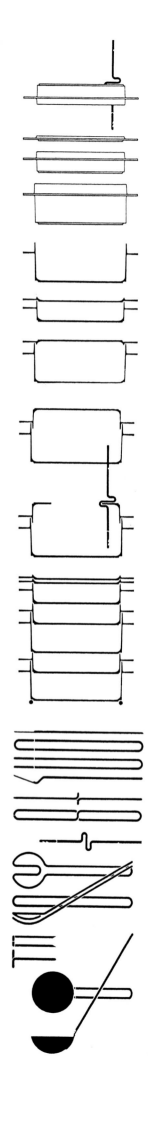

1

2

3

5

6

7

8

9

10

Georg Jensen, thermal carafe

The stainless steel, thermal carafe is the result of a long and unusual design process. It originated as a porcelain thermal carafe; part of a porcelain place setting designed for a competition. The organizer of the competition, Royal Copenhagen, found the proposal for the thermal carafe with a special closing mechanism, so original that they decided to develop it into a model suitable for production. As a result of the modeling process, porcelain proved to be an unfit material for the task. The rigorous dimensional tolerances of the porcelain shell could only be maintained with a great deal of difficulty. The closing mechanism – a ball in a self-closing lid, which automatically opens and closes with use – remained a promising and effective solution.

1

1. *Thermal carafe with a highly polished stainless steel finish.*
2. *The technical and functional attributes of the thermal carafe are synthesized into an aesthetic whole.*
3, 4, 5. *The closing mechanism is based upon a simple and original concept.*

The firm of Georg Jensen was interested in producing the thermal carafe in both stainless steel and plastic. This presented new demands on the project. Subsequently, only the main form's wide diameter and low centre of gravity were maintained. The closing mechanism concept was further developed to improve its functionality and suitability for production.

Following these changes, the lid could now be manufactured in two, cast plastic forms – the handle and the top in one part and the lid with closing mechanism in the other. The carafe is actually at rest when in pouring position, thus requiring less strength to pour. The material and harmonic form make the carafe aesthetically suited to almost all environments.

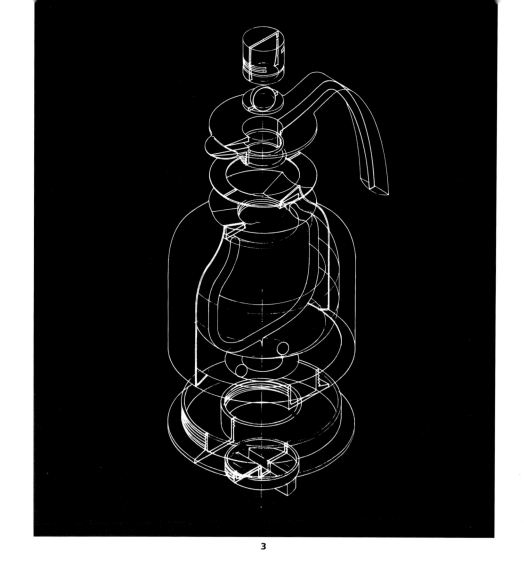

3

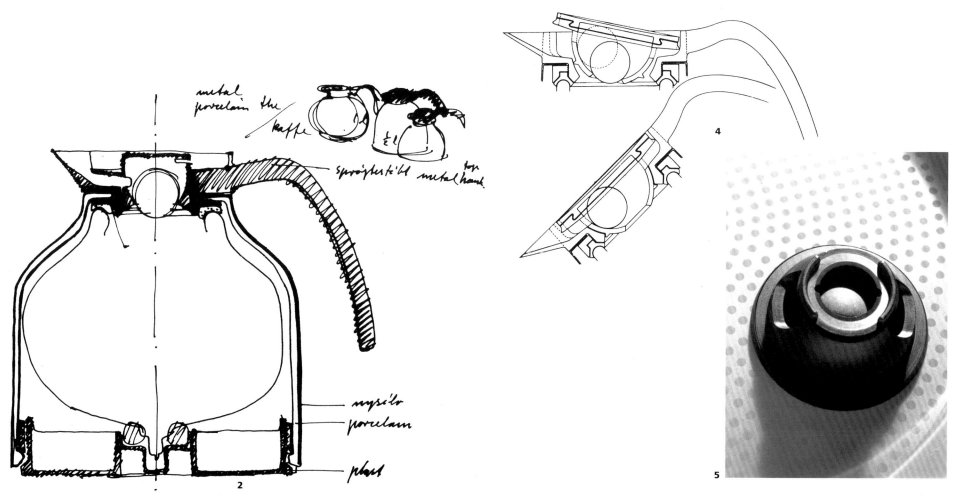

2

4

5

Stone Art, Club Manhattan

For the Dutch firm Stone Art, Knud Holscher designed a series of accessories for the serving of refreshments. Special consideration was given to the use of the Club Manhattan series in various situatios, for example on a garden terrace or on a boat. Consequently, all the pieces of the series are produced in a non-breakable, high quality plastic.

1

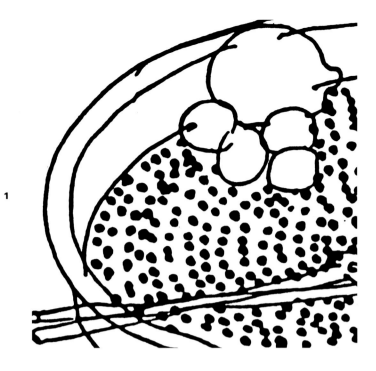

2

The series consists of pitchers, glasses, ice cube tongs, bottle openers, salt and pepper grinders, as well as two different sized serving trays. The classic modern design is refined in its simplicity and is presented with a brochure exclusively designed by Holscher's office.

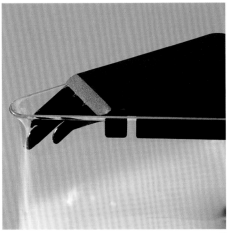

1. *Sketch.*
2. *One of the major design challenges was to create a comprehensive and corresponding relationship between all the pieces of the series. Club Manhattan creates a simple and beautiful setting for the informal serving of refreshments.*
3. *Ice bucket.*
4. *Pitcher, circular tray and glasses.*
5. *Pitcher lid detail.*

1–3. *Catalogue pages.*

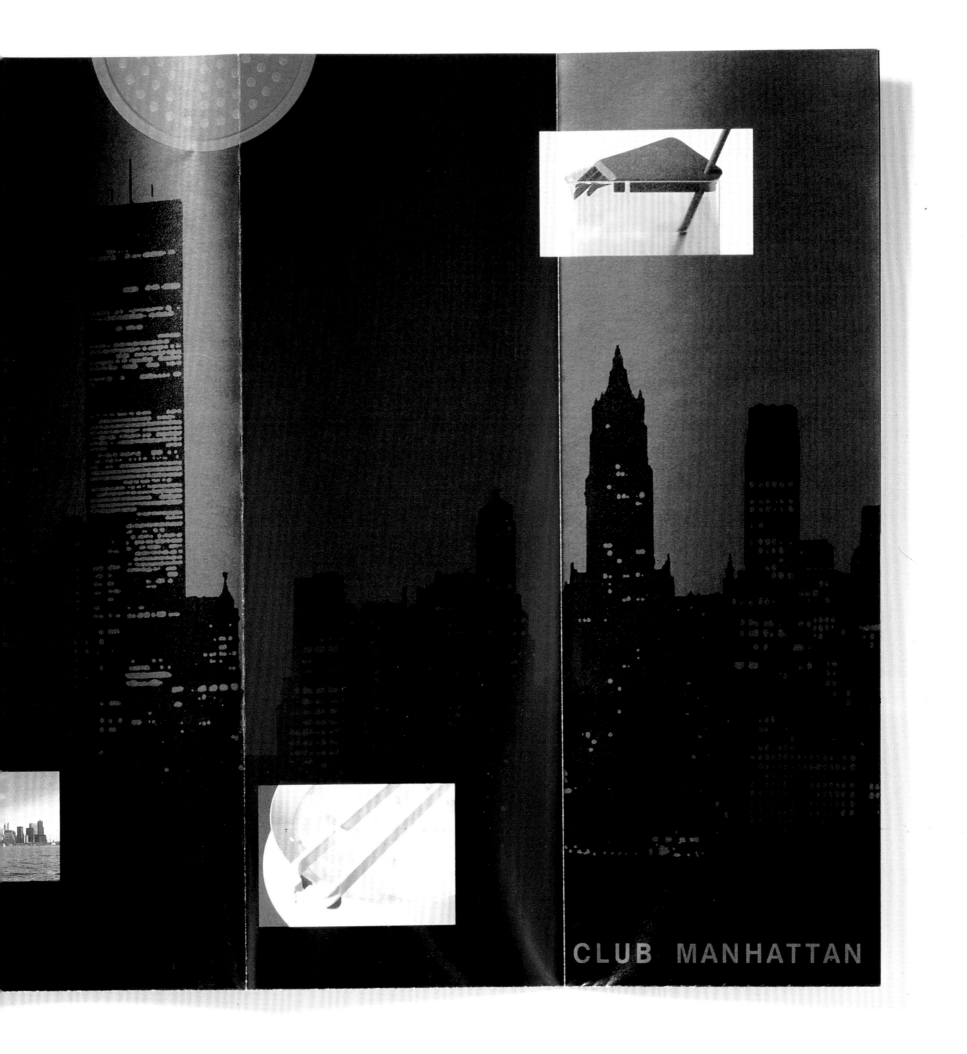

CLUB MANHATTAN

1

Illums Bolighus, bed system

Knud Holscher and Svend Axelsson devised a proposal for the design of a bed and night table for a competition written by Illums Bolighus. The two pieces could be arranged in various combinations to satisfy the requirements of reclining and sleeping, thereby, expanding the possible uses of a sleeping space.

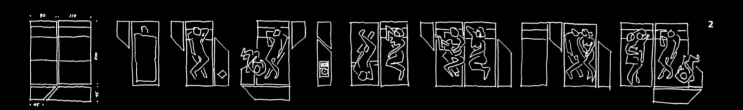

2

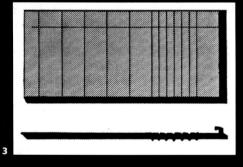

3

4

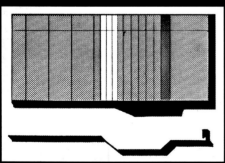

Dampa, ceiling system

In 1983, Dampa, a producer of suspended acoustic ceilings, sponsored a competition for the design of floors, walls, and ceilings that could be used to accommodate raw unfinished buildings. Knud Holscher Industrial Design won the competition with a proposal combining a limited number of aluminium wall and ceiling panel components that can be implemented into spaces of varying size, shape, and function. In addition,

there are components, which allow for the panels to be adapted to different corner, wall, and floor conditions. The Dampa system is equally suited for use as a suspended ceiling.

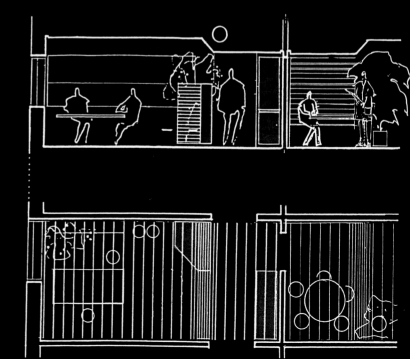

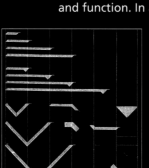

1. *Model.*
2. *Motion sketches.*
3, 4. *Formal variations of ceiling system.*
5. *Ceiling system profiles.*
6. *Possible applications of the system.*

Royal Copenhagen Porcelain

In 1983, Royal Copenhagen Porcelain wrote a competition calling for the design of a new, porcelain dinner set. For the competition, Knud Holscher created a design consisting of deep and flat plates and bowls. All setting pieces are designed to serve several purposes. For example, the plates can also be used as lids for the bowls; a practical solution for both the serving and refrigeration of food. A set of detachable rubber rings can be inserted between bowl and plate to ensure an airtight closure when refrigerating.

The competition project also contains a proposal for the design of a thermal, porcelain carafe.

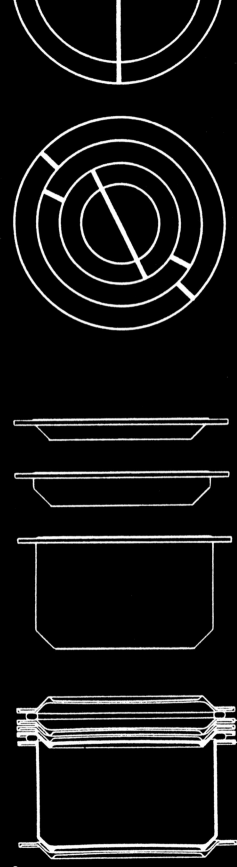

Facit io

The function of office organizations has changed with the introduction of new technologies. Workstations are increasingly the domain of computers. This has resulted in the need for new office furniture systems.

Facit io is a flexible and intelligent system of office furnishings consisting of relatively few components. The components can be combined to create innumerable configurations that accommodate the needs of both open plan and cellular office designs.

Programmed by the Englishman, Frank Duffy, the system consists of primarily five desk elements and a service wall element available in three heights. The Facit io system is based on a 60 cm module. The service wall elements enable the clear organization of office space for both individuals needing privacy or groups working in concert. The design of the desks furthers an efficient utilization of a space. They are organically formed, ergonomically determined, and adjustable in height. The system's aesthetics serve to break the monotony and uniformity that often characterize large, traditional office spaces.

The uniquely cost-effective design of the service walls accommodates and aesthetically conceals almost all electrical cabling needed. Using a wall rail system, overhead storage units and pinboards may be attached to the perimeter walls.

1. This office furniture system can be used for the planning of complete office landscapes, as well as the design of individual offices.
2. All components in the Facit io system permit the creation of an ergonomically correct workstation.
3–6. The backbone of the system is a service wall element that houses and conceals almost every cabling need, thus facilitating individual control of a workstation's lighting and H.V.A.C. needs.

2

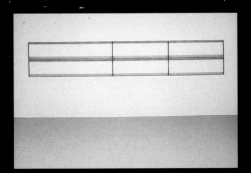

3

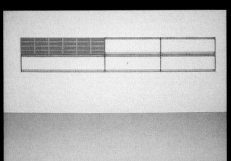

4

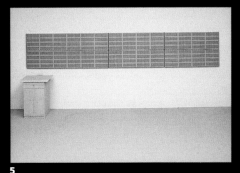

5

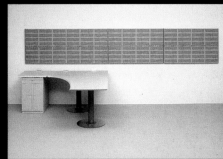

6

1

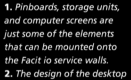

1. *Pinboards, storage units, and computer screens are just some of the elements that can be mounted onto the Facit io service walls.*
2. *The design of the desktop means a flexible and expedient utilization of space.*
3–10. *Building up system variations.*
11. *Detail.*
12, 13. *Office landscapes.*

Pages 100/101
14. *General view.*

2

3

4

5

6

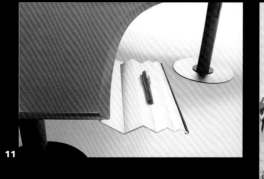

11

12

13

7

8

9

10

1. *General view.*
2. *Sketch.*
3–8. *The common task light fixture can be either built-in or suspended.*

1

Nordisk Solar, Triangel

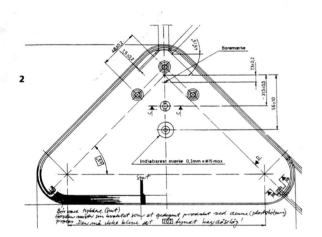

2

Thoughtful and appropriately designed lighting is a necessity to an effective working environment. Optimal, general lighting in working with computers demands the use of flexible fixtures. Based on the theories of the Austrian lighting expert, C. Bartenbach, the triangular fitting is designed with this purpose in mind.

Knud Holscher designed the fixture so that it can be integrated into either built-in or hanging systems. Triangel directs the light from its fluorescent tube by means of a reflector and louvre. The reflector can be either symmetrical or asymmetrical. When wall-mounted, the reflector is always closed. When hung as a pendant fixture, a reflector with an open topside can be used to illuminate the surface of the ceiling. The effect of the downward directed light is, however, consequently diminished.

To hang the expressive cast fixture, a suspension wire is secured to an integrated, wall-mounted fitting. It can then be adjusted to 0°, 45°, or 90°.

5

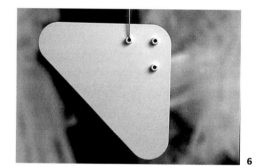

6

7

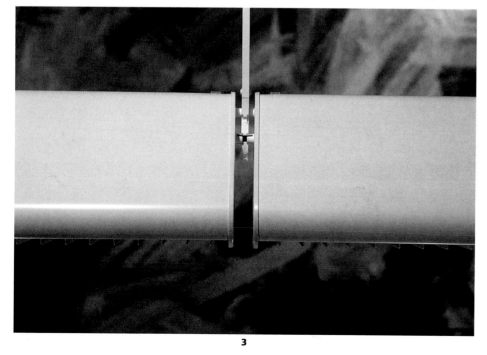

3

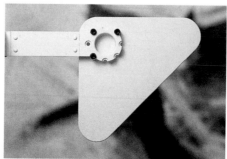

4

8

Coloplast, Assura

Complications with the digestive or urinary systems after an operation can make the use of a colostomy bag a necessity. It is of crucial importance that a colostomy bag be easy to use and that its user feels confident using the bag in public if a normal lifestyle is ever to be regained. The Assura colostomy bag was developed in close collaboration with nurses and patients. Special emphasis was placed on creating an intelligible, user-friendly means of operation that could be used by both the elderly and vision-impaired. With the press of a finger on a spring lock, the bag's connection ring is hermetically sealed.

Reception of the newly developed colostomy bag was so positive that for a long period of time supply could not meet demand.

1, 2, 4. *The closing mechanism is a decisive detail in the design of the Assura colostomy bag. It is both easy to operate and ensures that the bag is hermetically seal.*
3. *System drawing.*
5. *Sketch.*

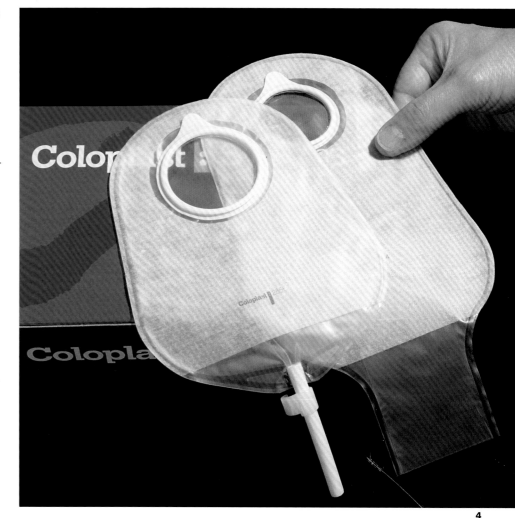

4

1

2

3

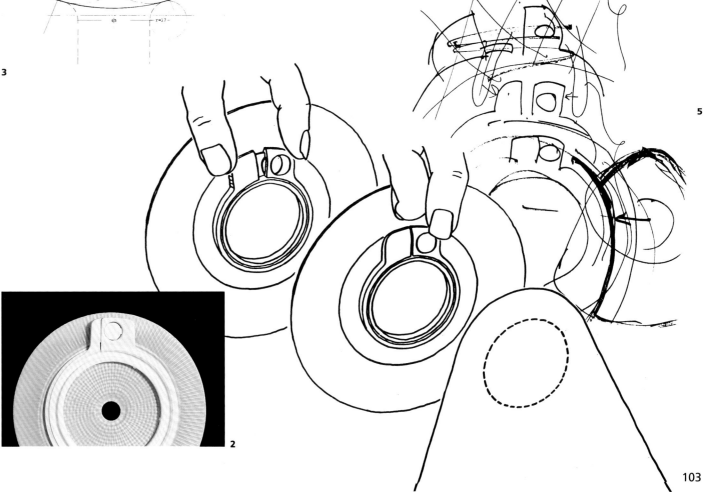

5

svrige oct 61 kHds

Part 6

2

1. *Water is both of practical and symbolic importance in the desert landscape of Bahrain.*
2. *The museum is designed in accordance with two modular grids, one of which is rotated 45° in relation to the other.*

Bahrain Civic Centre, Bahrain

Situated in the Persian Gulf, the Arabian emirate Bahrain is a small state comprised of eleven islands. It has developed into a modern nation, owing its wealth and prosperity to the oil industry. It was not until a couple of decades ago that there were any known reminders of the rich culture that had once thrived in Bahrain during the Bronze Age. The archeological excavations that took place from 1953–1965 under the direction of the Danish archeologist, P. V. Glob, unearthed the remains of a fortified city dating from the third century, BC. The numerous artifacts from that period confirm Bahrain's previous status as a wealthy centre of commerce.

At the end of the 1950s, in efforts to strengthen the small state's identity and pride, the Emir of Bahrain decided that a national museum should be erected in concert with the planning of a new civic centre. The scheme was also to include the design of the national library and a congressional centre with exhibition facilities. Following an international competition, the planning of the civic centre and the design of the museum were entrusted to Knud Holscher and Svend Axelsson, in collaboration with Cowi Consult. Without much hesitation, the Prime Minister decided that their winning proposal must be built.

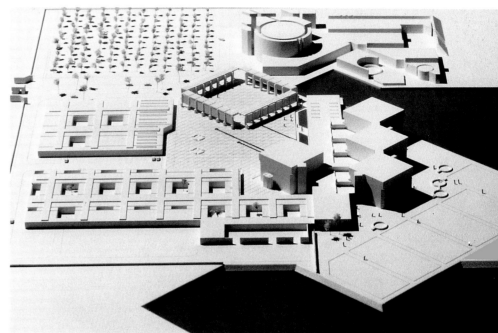

1

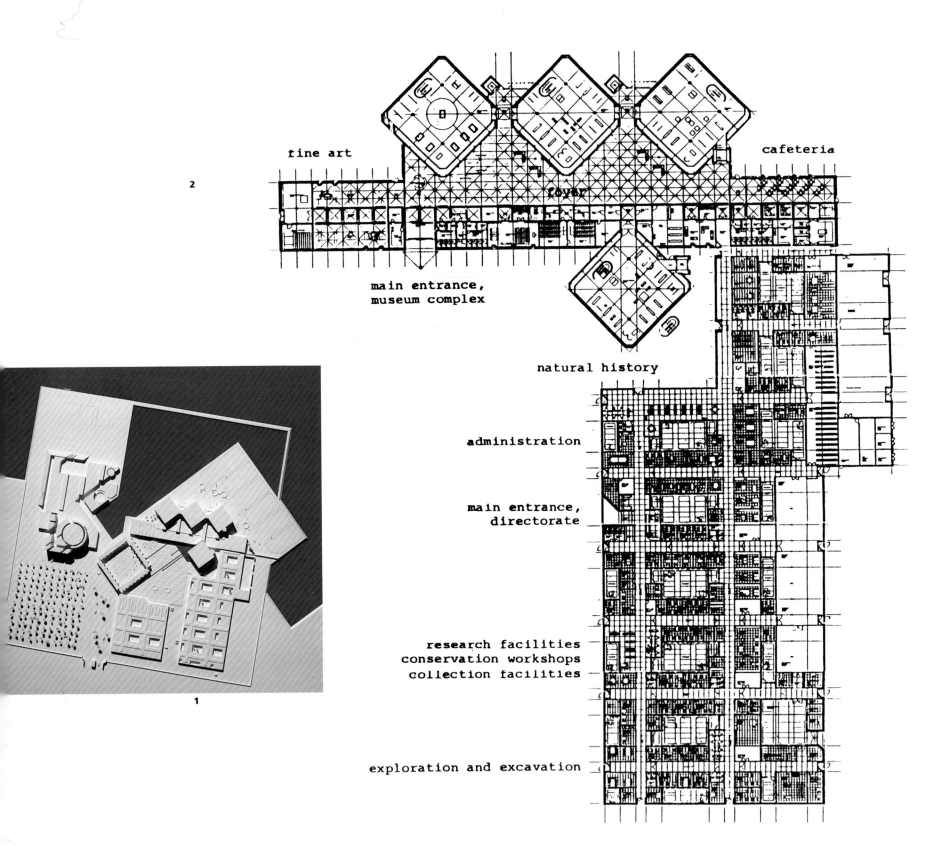

fine art

cafeteria

2

foyer

main entrance,
museum complex

natural history

administration

main entrance,
directorate

research facilities
conservation workshops
collection facilities

exploration and excavation

1

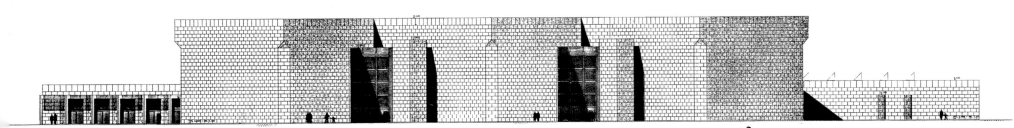

3

Based on the architects' proposal, the civic centre is sited on a back-filled peninsula. The museum accommodates a diverse program and is divided into two quadrants, one of which is rotated 45°. The one-storey buildings ordered within the first quadrant contain rooms for management, administration, research, and preservation. Two-storey, square blocks with space for galleries occupy the second quadrant. An embankment delimits a regulated basin, which serves as a reflecting foreground for the museum. The entire civic centre acts as a miniature Bahrain. It is framed by a wall that in combination with the basin's embankment wall forms a square. The simple, geometric organization of the plan and the placement of the individual buildings allude to traditional Islamic architecture.

1. *Because the site was artificially created, the site plan and buildings could be freely formed.*
2. *The museum's public galleries are characteristically different from the section of the building containing administration, archive, and research facilities.*
3. *Façade towards the reflecting basin.*
4. *An arcade creates an entry transition between city and museum.*
5. *Section through the public foyer.*

4

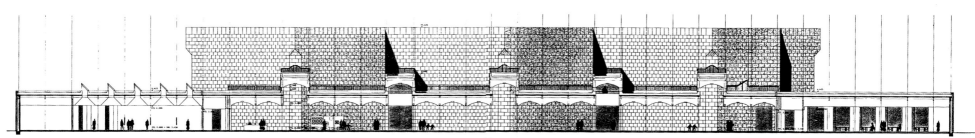

5

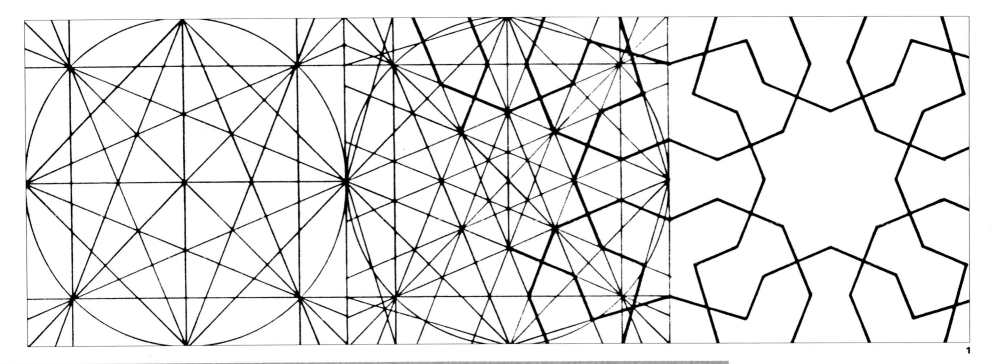

1

1, 3. *The evolution of an Arabic mosaic pattern is depicted on the walls of the museum.*
2. *Water as an environment-creating element is of vital importance to the Arabic building tradition.*
4, 5. *The benches are carved from massive blocks of travertine.*

2

3

Once inside the walls of the civic centre, there is just a short distance from the parking area to the planned congressional centre and square. The square is surrounded on all four sides by arcades, shielding it from the sun while simultaneously leaving it open to breezes coming from the Gulf. It serves as a meeting place, a forecourt or point of rotation, leading directly to the main entry of the museum and to the future facilities of the civic centre. The square is enriched by fountains, whose waters lead to the museum's reflecting basin.

The museum buildings are constructed of brick and clad in a travertine stone veneer. Both the marble tile floors in the foyer area and the interior, travertine walls have the colour of desert sand.

The exhibition spaces have wood floors. The patterns in the perforated aluminum screens were custom designed by the Holscher's office. The conscious limiting of material variations and the use of simple geometric forms establishes a homogeneity with Islamic building traditions.

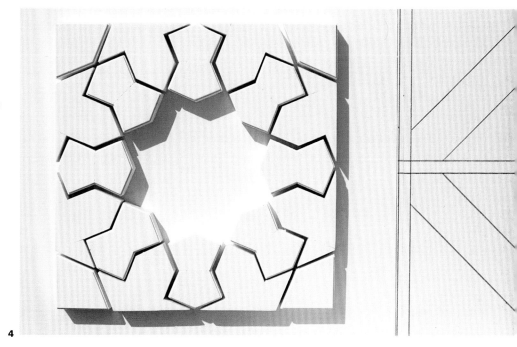

4

5

The intense, direct daylight characteristic of this latitude is minimized in response to both formal traditions and in order to moderate the interior climate of the buildings. The quadratic exhibition buildings are devoid of any fenestration so as to protect the artworks on display. However, there are interstitial spaces of pause located between every section of the museum, which provide views out towards the reflecting basin. The windowless portions of the building create a buffering effect, which supplemented with air conditioning equalize the difference between the low, night temperatures and the high, day temperatures.

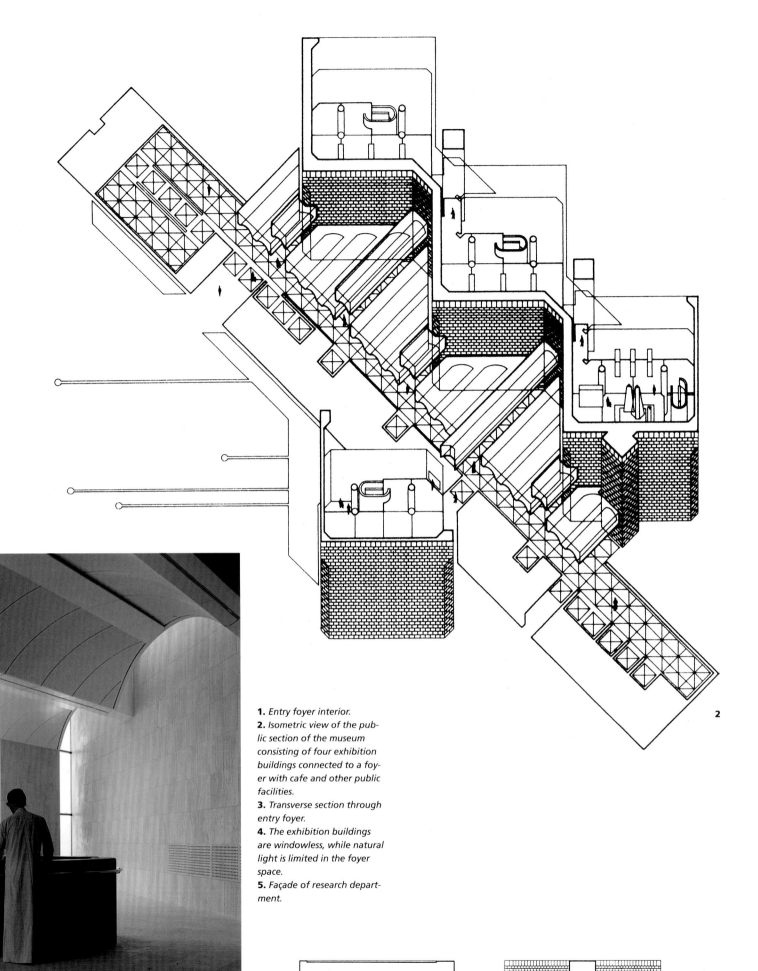

1. Entry foyer interior.
2. Isometric view of the public section of the museum consisting of four exhibition buildings connected to a foyer with cafe and other public facilities.
3. Transverse section through entry foyer.
4. The exhibition buildings are windowless, while natural light is limited in the foyer space.
5. Façade of research department.

1

2

3

4

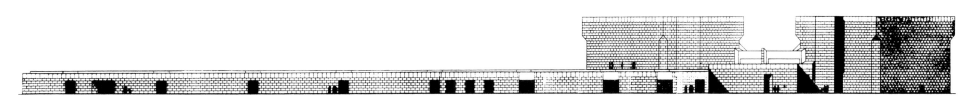

5

From the museum's large foyer, there is access to the various cultural collections, including pictorial art, archeology, ethnology, natural history, and technology. A wing housing class rooms and lecture halls forms the east wall of the foyer. The entire museum is designed with allusions to Islamic architecture, where the exhibition spaces create neutral frames around the displayed artifacts and artworks. The foyer is an architecturally ornate and expressive space. The roof consists of stepping, barrel vaults, which rest on concrete beams and are independent of the outer walls. This construction forms a band of natural, overhead light that filters down along the walls, accentuating the precisely carved mosaic patterns. The wall reliefs, as well as those adorning the floors, establish a strong affinity with traditional Islamic architecture. The colored, ceramic ornamentation in the research wing created by Bodil and Richard Manz further strengthens this adherence.

2

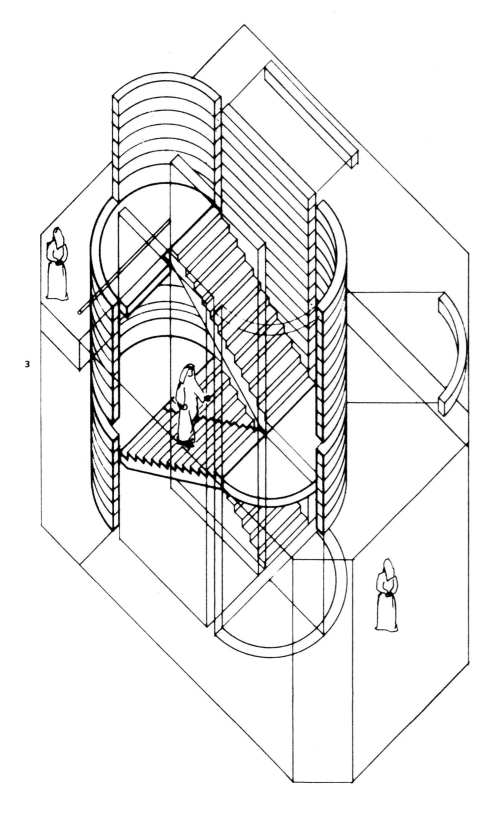

3

4

5

6

1. *Exhibition space in the archeological collection.*
2. *Exhibition space.*
3. *The stairwells in the exhibition buildings are designed to provide shifting views to the displayed works of art.*
4. *Stair detail.*
5. *Exhibition detail in the entry foyer.*
6. *Detail of ceramic artifact.*

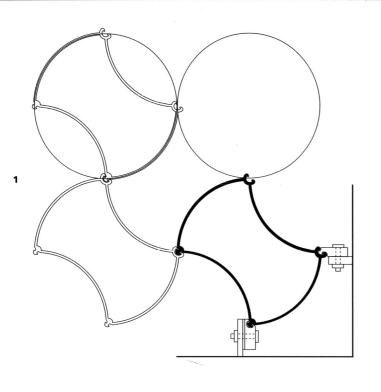

1

1. *Industrial design detail from the screens surrounding the quadrangle.*
2, 3. *Entry to the three, planned facilities occur via a formal, covered quadrangle.*

2

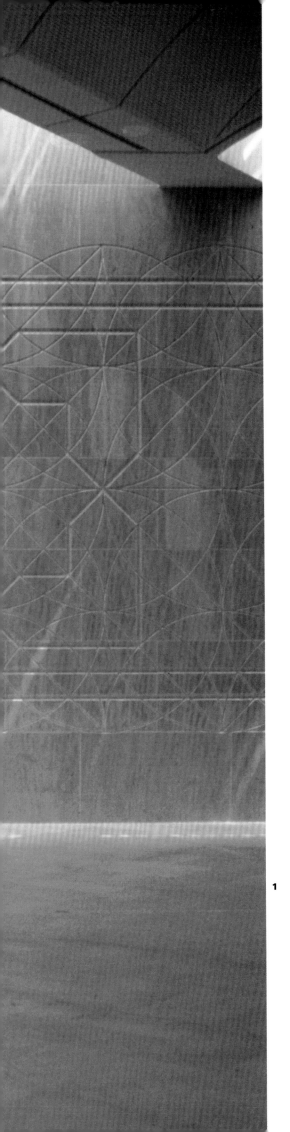

Like the atrium buildings, the one-storey buildings containing administrative offices, research facilities, and conservation workshops, are situated within a grid of adjoining walkways. Exterior walls of the buildings' wings have no windows facing their surroundings. The spaces receive light from the atrium courtyards, which with their artificial watering system act as small oasises in the subtropical climate. These courtyards also provide the possibility to individualize the various building sections based upon their different functions.

Torkild Ebert of the architecture firm, Thøgern & Ebert, was responsible for the design of the museum's display systems.

1

2

1. *Foyer interior.*
2. *The museum seen from Muharraq.*

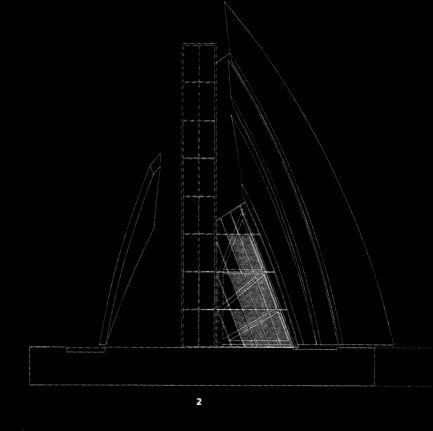

2

3

The Danish Pavilion, Expo '92, Seville

At the World Exposition in Seville, Denmark was represented by a pavilion that strove to express both the Danish landscape and new approaches in Danish architecture. The building was designed like a floating ship, with its massive white walls formed as sails and a central tower symbolizing a mast. The pavilion was a simple yet distinctive form, which clearly distinguished itself from the surrounding pavilions and secured much attention for Denmark. The project was the result of a design competition among five architects. The realized project was carried out with very few changes to the original concept. The design of the central space was based upon experience from previous expositions in Brussels and Montreal. Inside this space, there were seven large screens attached to the sail wall for the viewing of a huge audio-visual show depicting Danish art, culture, and economic life.

1, 3. *Entry towards the exhibition space. The large sails provided a much-welcomed, shaded reprieve from the intense heat of the Spanish summer.*
2. *Elevation.*
4. *The exterior walls of the exhibition hall are formed as 32 m high, white sails. They join a narrow 24 m high tower symbolizing a ship mast.*

1. *Exhibition space with audio-visual performance.*
2. *Model photo.*
3. *Plan.*
4. *The pavilion consisted of two main elements: a sail-formed outer wall and a modularly constructed administration building.*

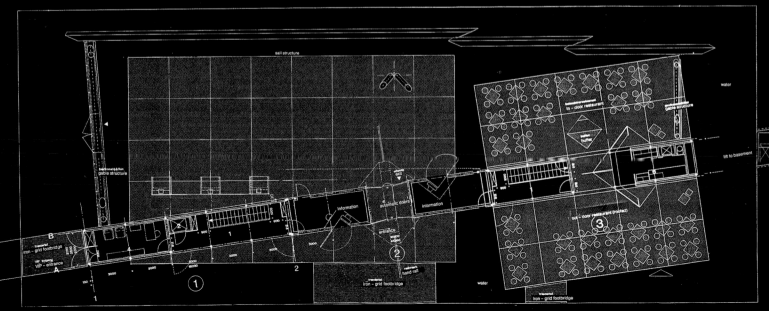

A method of construction incorporating lightweight, prefabricated components allowed the pavilion to be constructed in Denmark and transported to Seville for assembly.

Following this construction principle, the pavilion consisted of a large hall formed under the juncture of the metaphorical mast and sails. The long, tall mast building was constructed of lightweight frames clad in perforated sheet metal, and was completed with doors, windows, and walls. It housed conference rooms, toilets, offices, and staff rooms.

The sails were constructed of fibreglass reinforced plastic mounted on open-web girders, which were in turn supported by the mast building. The sails were sprayed throughout the day with water from the reflecting pool that surrounded part of the pavilion. Air intake along the base of the sail wall and powerful exhaust along the top was used to regulate the interior climate.

The individual components and the building, on the whole, were designed following an industrial design process based on computer-aided design. This also ensured that the building could endure exposure to the region's demanding climatic conditions.

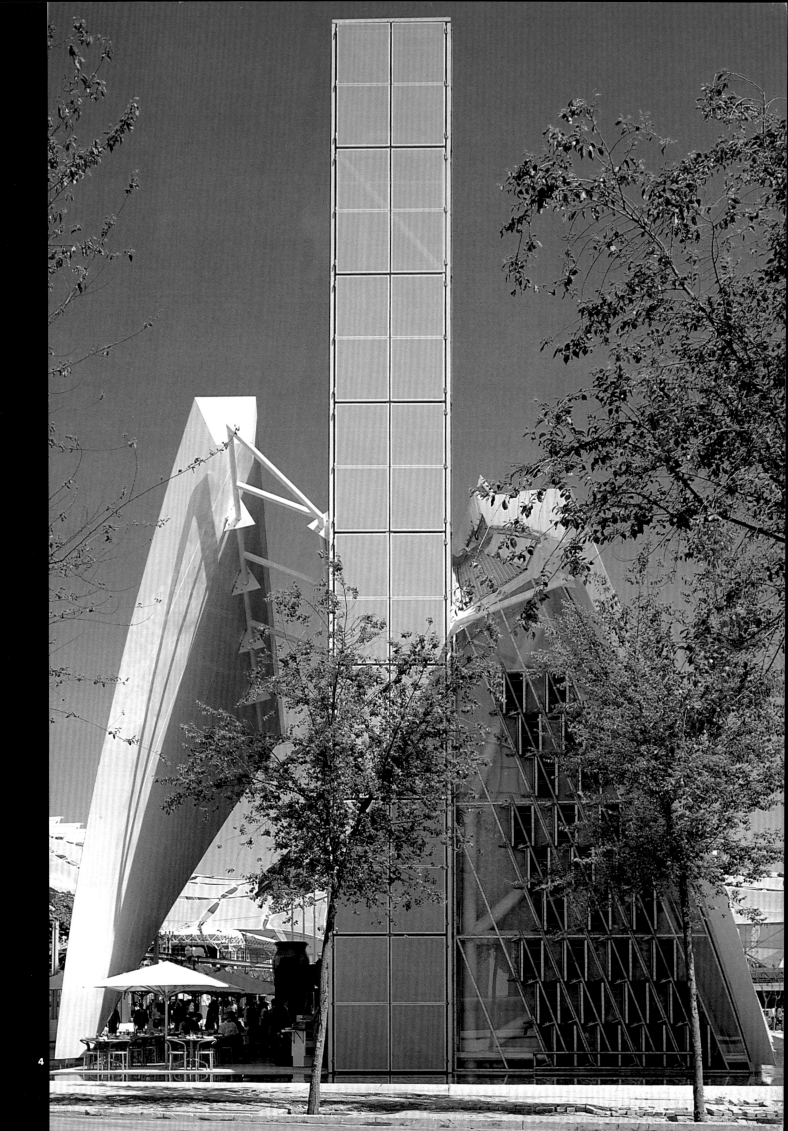

4

Knud Holscher's vacation house

Ordrup Næs is a narrow peninsula with a hilly terrain located in northwest Zealand. It consists primarily of small, naturally preserved areas. The remaining land is subdivided into a few, very large sites that ensure that the promontory is not over developed. Several years ago, Knud Holscher bought one of the sites with a small, primitive summerhouse sitting on it. The house was renovated and later a larger vacation house was built in order to establish a better dialogue with the natural attributes of the site and its many admirable views.

The new vacation house is approximately 100 sqm and is erected in harmoney with the existing tranquility of the site.

The house is a simple stud-frame construction with a lightweight roof. Entry to the house occurs via the north and south walls, which are formed as deep, windowless niches. The north wall contains the kitchen fixtures and appliances, while the south wall houses storage cabinets.

The exterior wall of the bathroom core is brick. The remaining exterior walls are glass, providing unrestricted views to the sea and Nexelø from the main spaces of the house. The ceiling is slightly vaulted and clad in birch panelling, with skylights occurring over the kitchen and living areas. The floors are also of wood.

1. *View of the vacation house seen from the north.*
2. *The interior visually merge with the surrounding landscape.*
3. *Ground plan.*
4. *View of the vacation house seen from the south.*

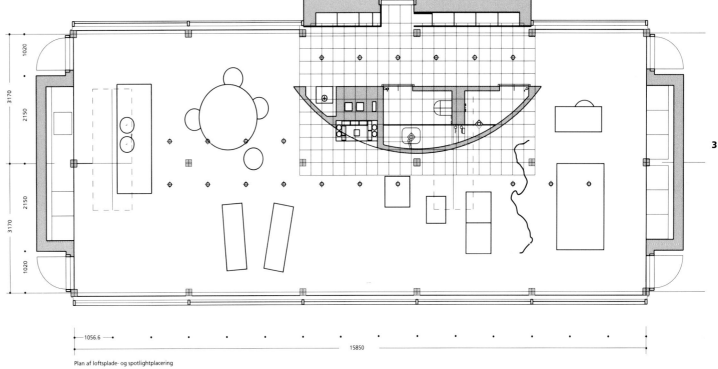

3

1056.6

15850

Plan af loftsplade- og spotlightplacering

4

Except for the shielded portion of the kitchen and the rounded wall of the bathroom core, the house has no dividing walls. The furniture alone serve to divide the space into dining, living, and sleeping areas. Children's bedrooms are located in the renovated summerhouse.

A system of decks defines the exterior spaces on both the north and south sides of the house. Both the decks and the interior floors are elevated 40 cm higher above grade. The surrounding, natural vegetation extends directly up to the house's periphery, visually bridging house and landscape.

126

1. *Vacation house seen from the south.*
2. *Bedroom interior.*
3, 4. *Detail of the surrounding, timber terraces which bridge the house to the verdant surrounds.*

Part 7

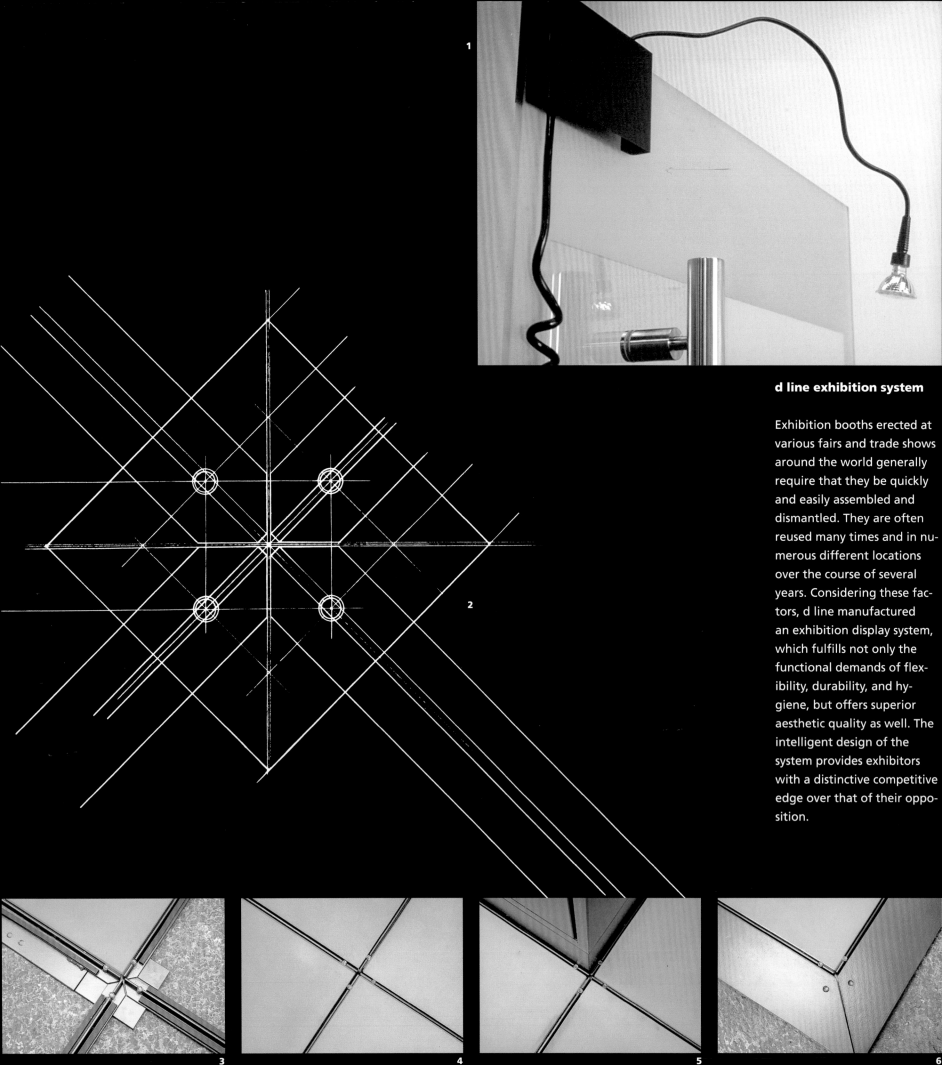

1

2

3

4

5

6

d line exhibition system

Exhibition booths erected at various fairs and trade shows around the world generally require that they be quickly and easily assembled and dismantled. They are often reused many times and in numerous different locations over the course of several years. Considering these factors, d line manufactured an exhibition display system, which fulfills not only the functional demands of flexibility, durability, and hygiene, but offers superior aesthetic quality as well. The intelligent design of the system provides exhibitors with a distinctive competitive edge over that of their opposition.

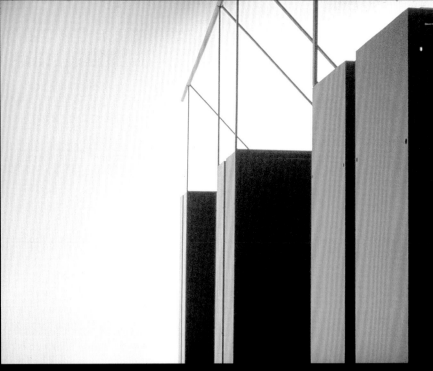

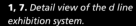

9

The d line system is based on a series of modular metal profiles, which are laid out in grids on the floor to define the extent of the booth/ exhibition area. The profiles are then, in turn, used to support glass plates that form the system's walls and display cases. If desired, storage units and lighting fixtures can also be mounted harmoniously onto the wall panels. A ceiling covers the entire booth layout, providing continuity of the exhibition and restraining the possible damage caused by smoke and flames in the event of a fire.

d line International typically contracts different architecture and interior design firms to plan the layout of the booths/ exhibition areas. In order to increase the accuracy and efficiency of designing and calculating each project, the components of the d line exhibition system have been incorporated into an IT-program that can be combined with the CAD drawings of the architects and manufacturers. Once a layout has been approved, the design firm simply formulates an inventory list of the required components, and then d line International packages and ships the parts directly to the fair location for installation.

10

11

8

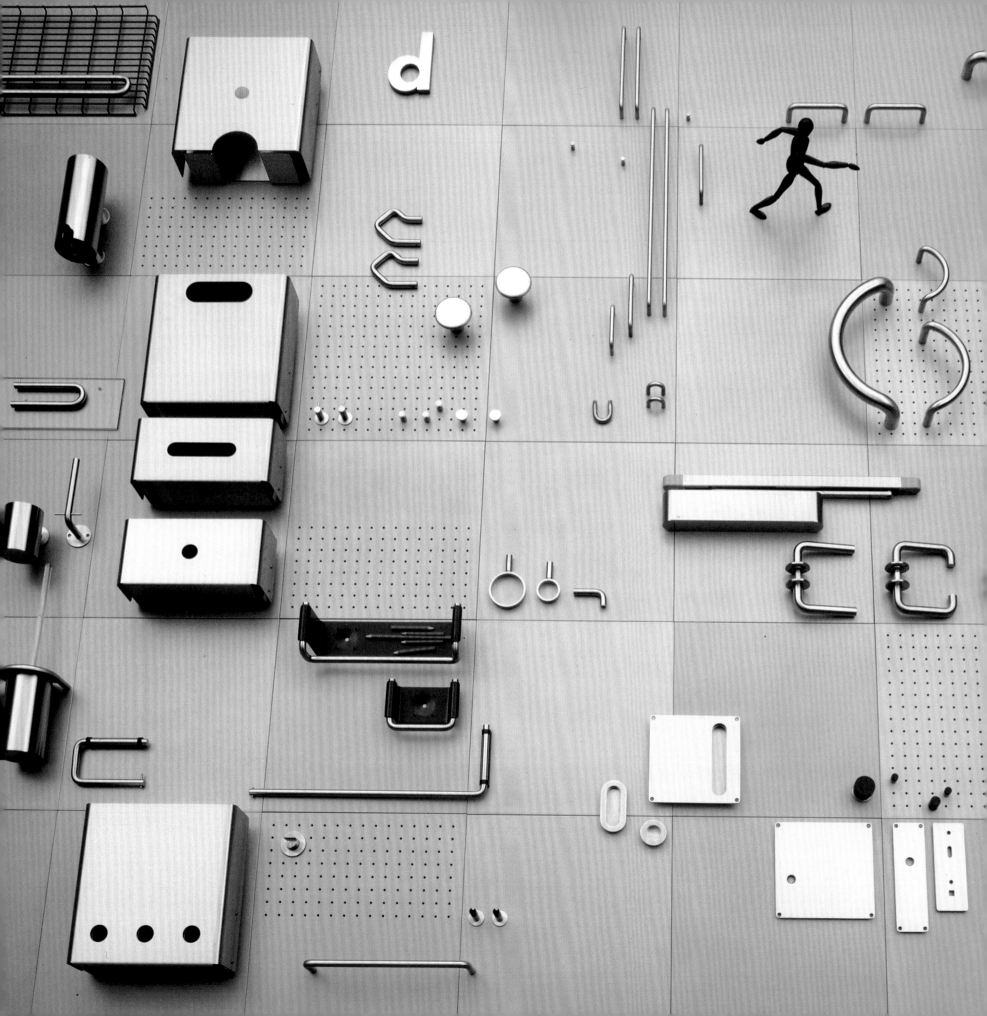

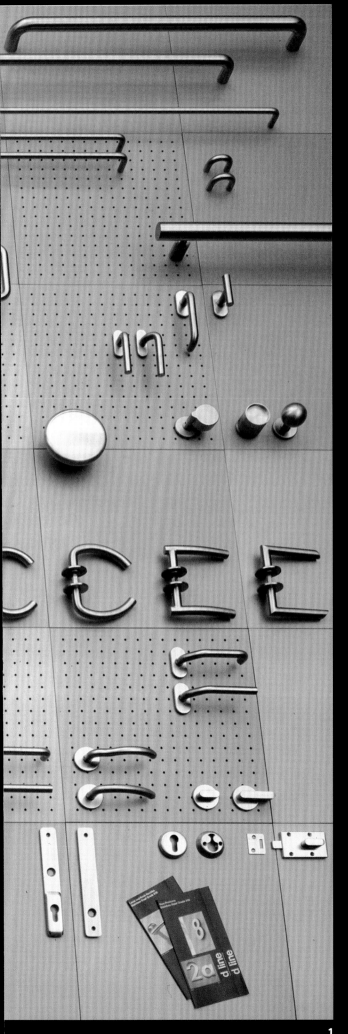

The d line family

d line is built upon the idea of creating visually, interrelated building fittings that enable a space to be perceived as a unified whole. Over the course of several years, the d line series has grown, with new products still being added to date. The new fittings are typically categorized according to the functional areas in which they will be installed, for example under commercial, residential, or industrial environments.

1. *d line items.*
2. *Sanitary exhibition unit.*
3. *Address number.*

d line, built-in sanitary panel system

The built-in sanitary system consists of 10 different functional modules that can be combined in numerous varieties according to needs.

1. *d line's built-in sanitary panel system is a highly flexible modular concept designed for use in a variety of applications; primarily toilet cubicles, washrooms, and kitchenettes. The system is produced in acid resistant stainless steel and can be installed either horizontally or vertically via a special universal mounting frame, thus making it appropriate for commercial, industrial, and residential environments. Waste paper bin, plastic bag, paper towel and paper cup dispensers are just a few of the modules available. There are ten different modules in all, which can be combined based upon desire and requirement.*

2–4. *Mounting sequence of a vertical, sanitary panel. The modules are installed into a recessed, pre-fabricated frame and are then locked into place with the use of a concealed communal locking system located at the base of the frame. The height of the panel depends upon the chosen combination. Here, hand dryer, soap dispenser, paper towel dispenser, and waste paper bin are combined for use in a public washroom.*
5. *A vertical section through the panel system demonstrates the tilting lid mechanism and automatic snap-lock that make it virtually effortless to refill and empty, or even replace the individual modules.*
6. *A vertical combination containing toilet seat cover dispenser, tissue and toilet paper dispensers, and waste bin suitable for use in a public washroom, among other spaces.*

2

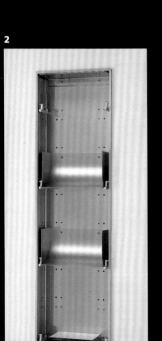

3

4

6

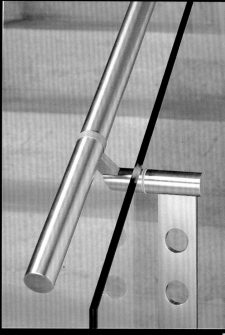

2

3

d line, balustrade and handrail system

The balustrade and handrail system is based upon the idea of "clever" junctions and "trivial" tubes to cater for the majority of architectural conditions.

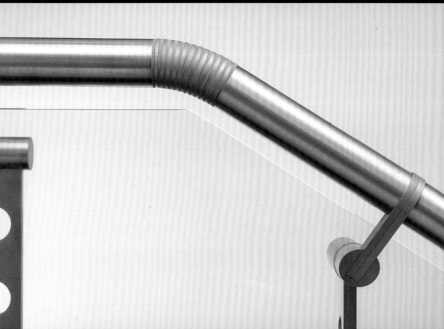

1

1. The balustrade and handrail system consists of a series of approximately twenty newly developed components. Among these is a unique "flexible elbow" joint that makes it possible to adjust the handrail on-site to fit a diversity of stair conditions and gradients.

2. The balustrade's infill walls are of tempered, laminated glass.

3. The handrail, glass infills, and upright brackets are joined via a specially developed grub screw and expansion cone system, incorporating blasted stainless steel washers and UV stabilized thermo plastic rubber washers. All of the system's elements are dimensioned in accordance with current EU specifications and standards.

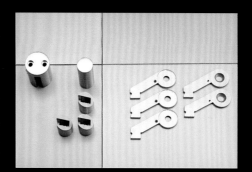

4

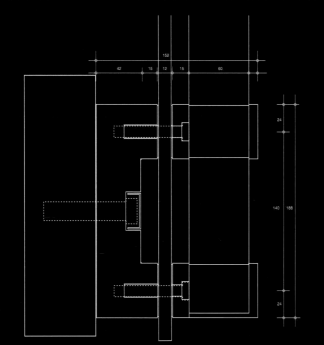

4. The "building components" make it possible to assemble and dismantle the balustrade and handrail system in sequence.

5. Joining of upright bracket and infill to side of the stairway flight with the help of a special footing socket. The assembly sequence has been optimized through intensive design development.

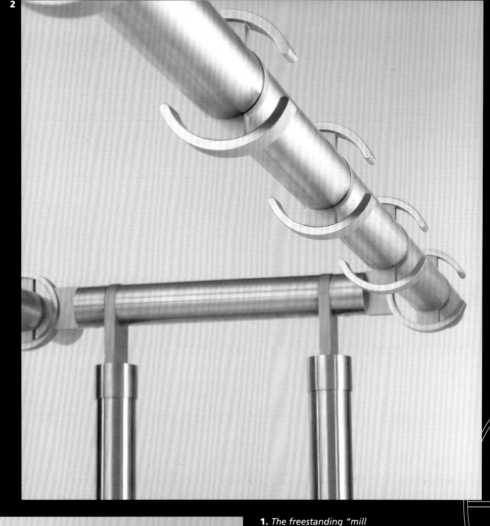

The cloakroom system consists of a number of very detailed cast stainless steel components that can be combined to fulfill a great variety of applications.

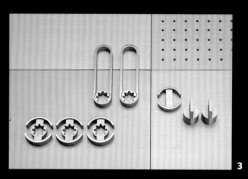

1. The freestanding "mill wheel" hat and coat rack is also equipped with an umbrella stand. Here, cast coat and hat hooks are mounted to a flat stainless steel ring.

2. This sample combination is well suited for use in theatre foyers, among several other public spaces.

3. The cloakroom system is based upon a series of fourteen different items components, which are combined with 38 mm steel tubes to satisfy a variety of applications. All components are of acid resistant stainless steel and are available in either satin or glass blasted finishes.

4. The freestanding "signpost" model has rotating coat and hat hooks that can be adjusted to fulfill a diversity of needs.

Plan

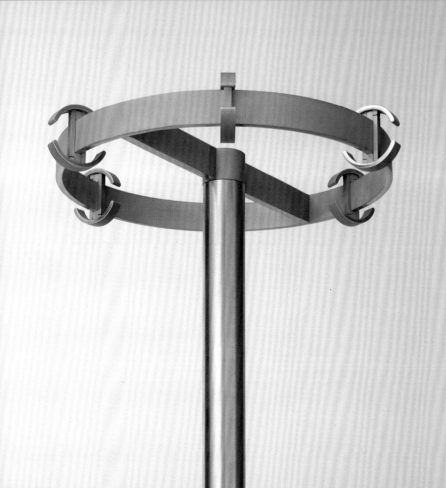

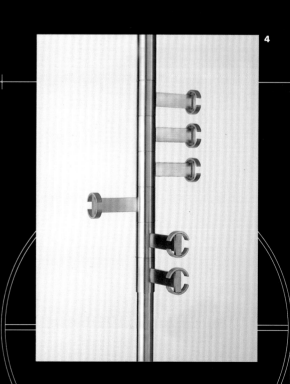

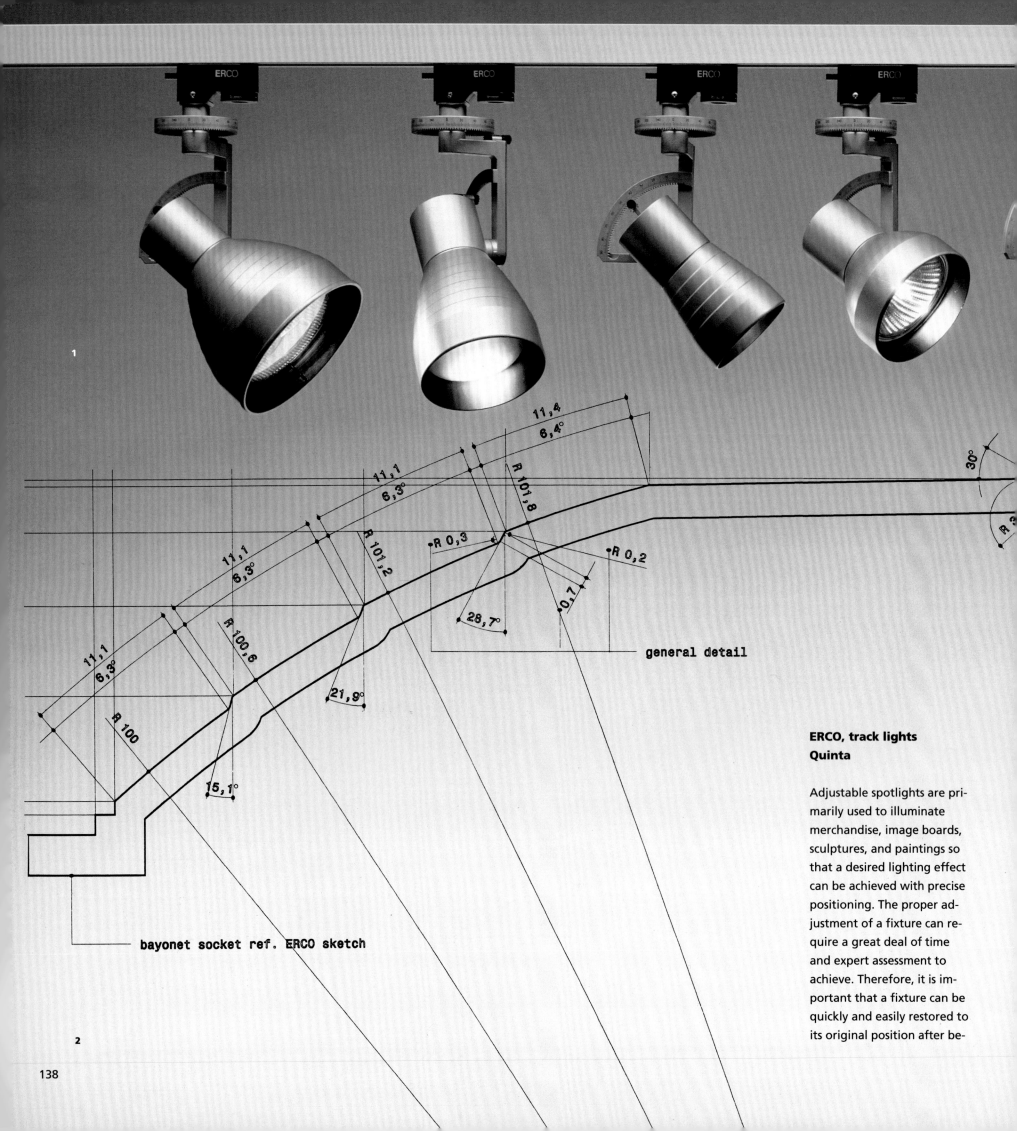

11,4
6,4°

11,1
6,3°

R 101,8

30°

R 101,2

R 0,3

R 0,2

11,1
6,3°

0,7

28,7°

general detail

R 100,6

21,9°

11,1
6,3°

R 100

15,1°

bayonet socket ref. ERCO sketch

ERCO, track lights
Quinta

Adjustable spotlights are primarily used to illuminate merchandise, image boards, sculptures, and paintings so that a desired lighting effect can be achieved with precise positioning. The proper adjustment of a fixture can require a great deal of time and expert assessment to achieve. Therefore, it is important that a fixture can be quickly and easily restored to its original position after be-

1

2

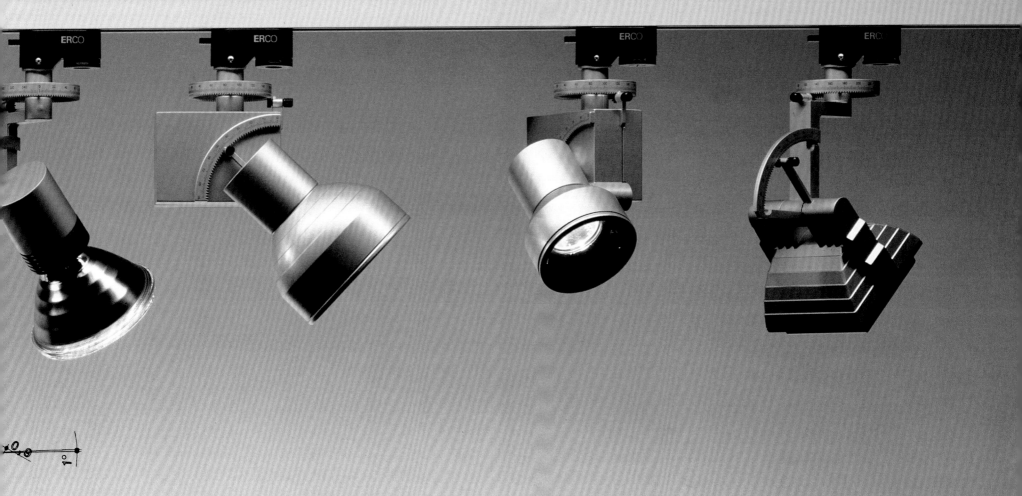

ing removed or readjusted in conjunction with cleaning or maintenance. Knud Holscher Industrial Design designed a series of fifteen spotlights for ERCO. Although the series elaborates upon a previous series created by an Italian designer, Quinta is a new design in itself.

Quinta spotlights are suspended in an electrical track making them easy to relocate and reposition. Angle of inclination dials make them simple to return to their appropriate positions in the event that they become unaligned for one reason or another. Each fixture is equipped with both horizontal and vertical dials. The horizontal dial is circular and has a full graduation of 360°. The vertically positioned dial is only a quarter-circle with an indication

range from 0° to 90°. Together, they verify the specific inclination angle of a spotlight in the x, y, and z directions. The reflector's position is also confirmed on the dials, and can be moved horizontally, vertically, or locked into a set position. It is therefore always easy to specify or record the correct angle of a spotlight. This technique can be compared with that of a sextant used to secure the course and position of a ship.

The superior craftsmanship that is characteristic of an instrument maker's work served as a model for the Quinta series. Both the fixture's suspension arm and housing are produced in cast aluminium. The housing is an intelligent and expressive form. The reflector can be used with tungsten halogen,

low-pressure halogen, and compact fluorescent lamps. A reflector for use with floodlights is also available.

ERCO's owner, Klaus Jürgen Maack, who is a respected figure in the German design world proved an inspiration throughout the course of the series' evolvement. All of ERCO's products are simply yet expressively formed with a great deal of attention being given to their functionality and durability.

ERCO track lights have been granted the German Design Award, the IF Prize, and Düsseldorf Design Zentrum's Rote Punkt Award.

3

1. *Adjustable spotlights from the Quinta series.*
2. *System drawing.*
3. *Detail of a spotlight from the Quinta series showing the horizontal and vertical dials.*

ERCO, Zenit Uplight

Zenit is a bowl-shaped fixture that combines indirect ambient lighting with direct task lighting. When illuminating spaces with VDU workstations, special attention must be paid to the luminary balance between the surrounding space and the information being displayed on the computer screens. This balance is too often incidental due to inexpedient general lighting designs, and results in problems of glare and reflection.

Zenit emits a controlled downward light that supplies a moderate and well-balanced general light, guaranteeing visual comfort and minimizing the effects of glare. The downward light projected off the underside of two wing reflectors may be advantageous, for example in a conference room, but proves crucial in the illumination of working surfaces. By

simply re-positioning the reflectors, the fixture doubles as a task light. The result of this feature is a remarkably uniform lighting arrangement with additional task lighting being provided directly to a working plane.

Zenit luminaires are available as freestanding, pendant, or wall-mounted.

1

3

1. *Quinta spotlight with adjustable barn doors.*
2. *Zenit design development sketch.*
3. *Freestanding version of Zenit luminaire.*

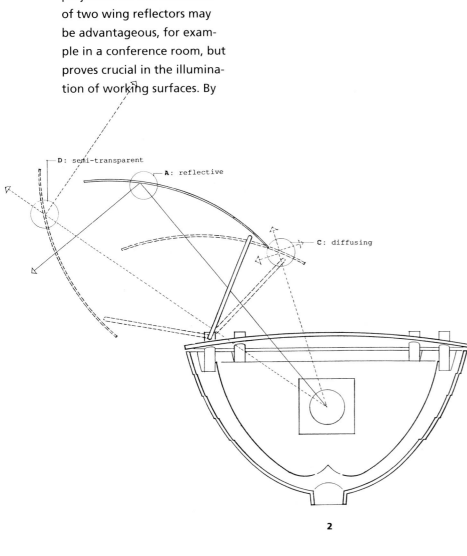

D: semi-transparent

A: reflective

C: diffusing

2

1

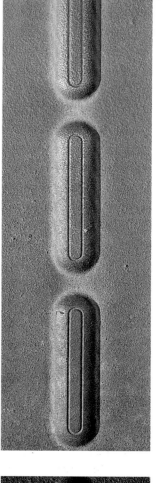

2

GH form, Pictoform

In collaboration with Landscape architect Charlotte Skibsted and various institutes for the blind, Knud Holscher developed a system to help the blind and visually impaired find their way more easily when walking about the city. In principle, the system consists of a series of elements, which can be inserted into the city's sidewalks and other ground surfaces.

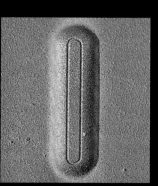

The elements are designed as a series of guidelines. Each element is equipped with raised tactile symbols; dashed lines indicate direction, while angles and crosses signify changes in direction. Other tactile symbols indicate, for example the location of bus stops or warn against oncoming traffic. There are sixteen different sized elements, which can be produced in either cast iron, concrete, or bronze. This system can be adapted to all types of walking surfaces, but was envisioned as being for use in areas of the city where the blind and vision-impaired walk the most.

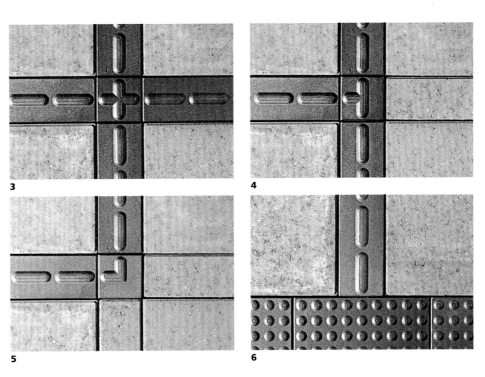

3

4

5

6

7

1. *Cast iron pavers with slightly raised bumps serve as tactile, directional indicators that the blind can easily follow with the use of a cane. (Copenhagen Town-Hall Square.)*
2. *Detail photo of guiding paver elements in cast iron.*
3–7. *Various pavers with directional and cautionary bumps.*
8. *Detail of a caution paver.*

8

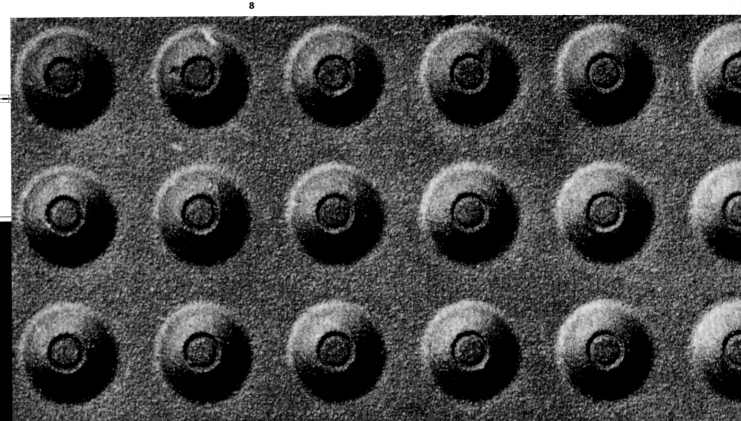

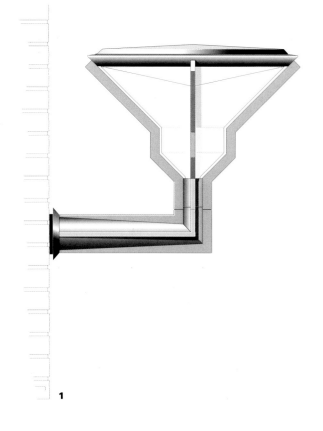

1

GH form, cast-iron street lamps

Over the course of several years, cast iron has been one of the preferred materials for the production of street furniture. Its manufacturing process is simple and it is a strong, maintainence-free, recyclable material. Despite its positive attributes, cast iron was displaced for quite some period of time by other materials.

Cast iron's admirable qualities are one of the reasons for its rediscovery in the production of modern street furniture. Its historical background remains yet another. GH form, a small iron foundry located in Holbæk, commissioned Knud Holscher to design a cast iron street lamp. It was to be specifically used in a part of the old, historically preserved district of Odense. However, the street lamp was also to be designed so that it could be erected in all urban environments where an integration between modern street lighting and historically preserved buildings was desired.

The street lamp that resulted from the collaboration with GH form has a solid, cast pole, formed like a column with flanges tapering upwards towards the housing of the lantern. The column is widest at its base in order to accommodate the connection and service of the electrical supply.

The design of the lantern's housing has four ribs that can be seen as extensions of the column's flanges. A top ring secures the ribs in their proper position. The lantern is shaped like a funnel resting between the four ribs. Covered by a circular lid, the housing is so spacious that several different types of lampsource can be used depending upon the projected budget and the desired color and intensity of the light. A reflector under the lid directs the light downwards where it is most needed. This is both an economic advantage and a sensitive response to the city's lighting environment.

Moreover, an L-shaped bracket was designed for wall-mounting the lantern. This enables it to be used regularly on the narrow streets characteristic of the older parts of the city. The design of the street lamp is modern, yet makes clear references to traditional street furniture. It is an aesthetically refined element, which graciously promotes the transition between old and new in historic city environs.

Knud Holscher also created a bollard for the purpose of defining the boundaries between the city's vehicular and pedestrian spaces. The bollard is constructed in cast iron and is formally related to the design of the street lamps. It is available in two heights, with one of the models being equipped with a glass top section in which a luminary can be installed.

2

3

1. *Wall-mounted version of cast iron street lamp.*
2. *Erection of a street lamp prototype in Odense.*
3. *Cast iron street lamps used in front of Sønderborg Castle in Jutland, Denmark.*
4. *High and low bollards employed on a cobble-stone square.*
5. *Detail of bollard top.*
6. *The bollard series consists of:*
– grade level bollard, directional markers, used for example to indicate the division of parking spaces;
– low bollard;
– high bollard;
– high bollard with glass top and lamp.
7. *High bollard with glass top and lamp.*

4

5

7

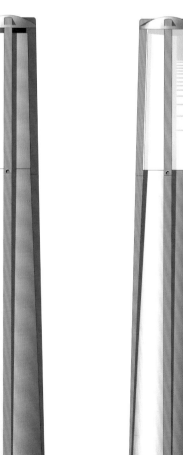

6

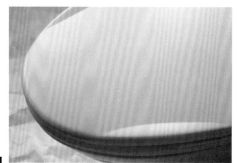

1. *Pressalit seat cover.*
2. *The softly curved forms of the toilet bowl.*
3, 4. *The classic lines of the wash basin result from a strict adherence to geometric principles.*

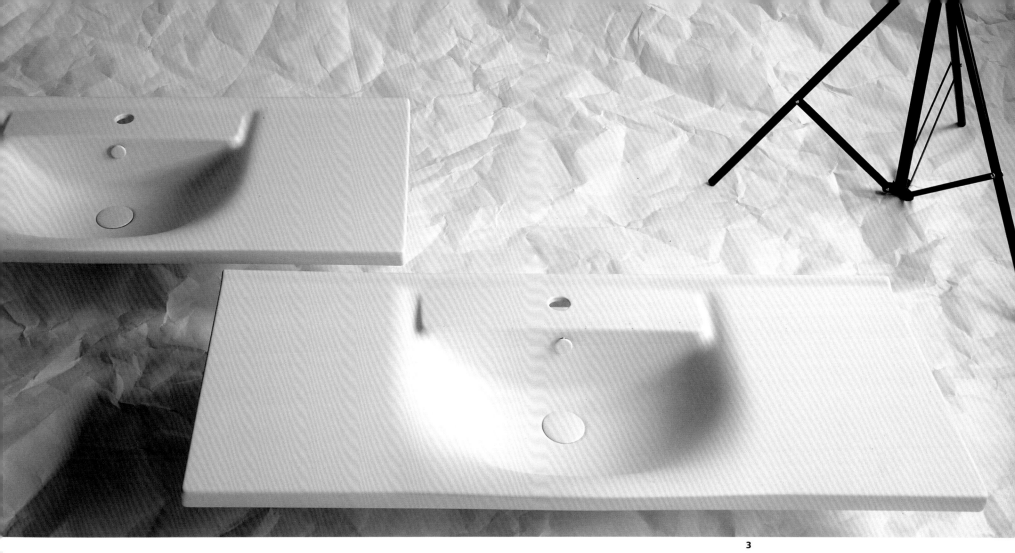

3

IFÖ, Cerenova

Cerenova is a new generation of sanitary porcelain produced by the Swedish firm, IFÖ. In the developmental phase of the work, the practical needs of cleaning and maintenance were just as decisive to the design as aesthetic intentions. The rounded, organic forms create a congruous interplay with the proportions of the human body, as well as being pleasing to the eye.

A glazed interior surface and a wider rim opening are just a few of the technical improvements made to the design of the toilet bowl. These modifications ease cleaning and prevent calcification of the bowl. In addition, the water closet's connection to the floor and the joint between the cistern and the bowl have also been hygienically and aesthetically improved.

The design of the new lavatory has an even more elegant expression. The shallow design of the basin reflects considerations of the fact that running water is most often used when washing hands or brushing teeth. Several smaller changes have also been introduced, for example a so-called half column has been designed to conceal the drain trap and soil pipe.

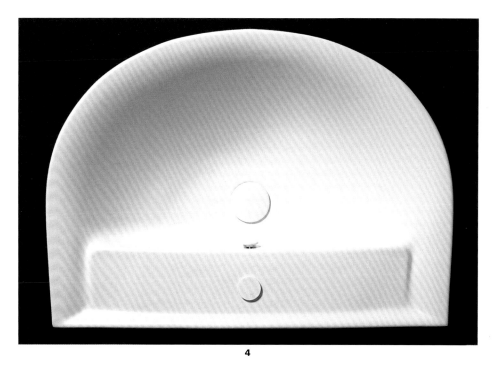

4

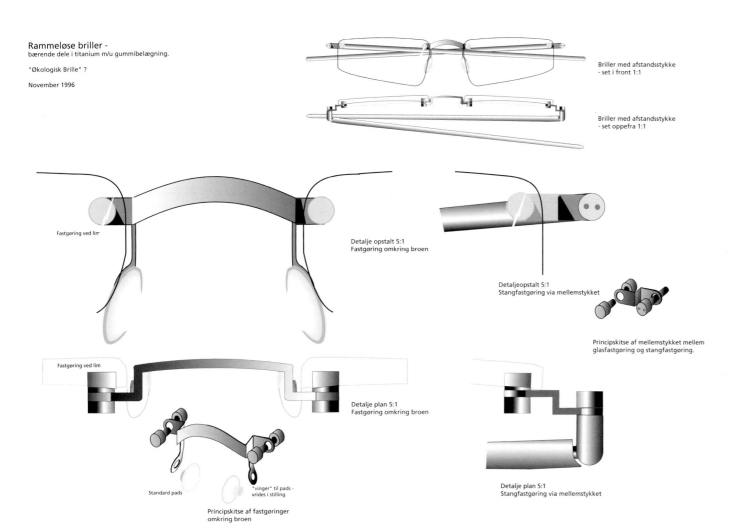

Rammeløse briller -
bærende dele i titanium m/u gummibelægning.

"Økologisk Brille" ?

November 1996

Briller med afstandsstykke
- set i front 1:1

Briller med afstandsstykke
- set oppefra 1:1

Fastgøring ved lim

Detalje opstalt 5:1
Fastgøring omkring broen

Detaljeopstalt 5:1
Stangfastgøring via mellemstykket

Principskitse af mellemstykket mellem
glasfastgøring og stangfastgøring.

Fastgøring ved lim

Detalje plan 5:1
Fastgøring omkring broen

Standard pads

"vinger" til pads -
vrides i stilling

Principskitse af fastgøringer
omkring broen

Detalje plan 5:1
Stangfastgøring via mellemstykket

Eyeglasses

Despite the simple task and
function of supporting two
optical lenses, the design of
eyeglass frames has always
tempted many designers.
Knud Holscher Industrial Design proposed a pair of glasses without frames for the
lenses, thus minimizing dis-
turbances of one's facial features as much as possible.
The frames are simple and
"technically" formed so that
the glasses can stand up to
everyday use. The design of
these eyeglasses was a developmental project, which was
never realized.

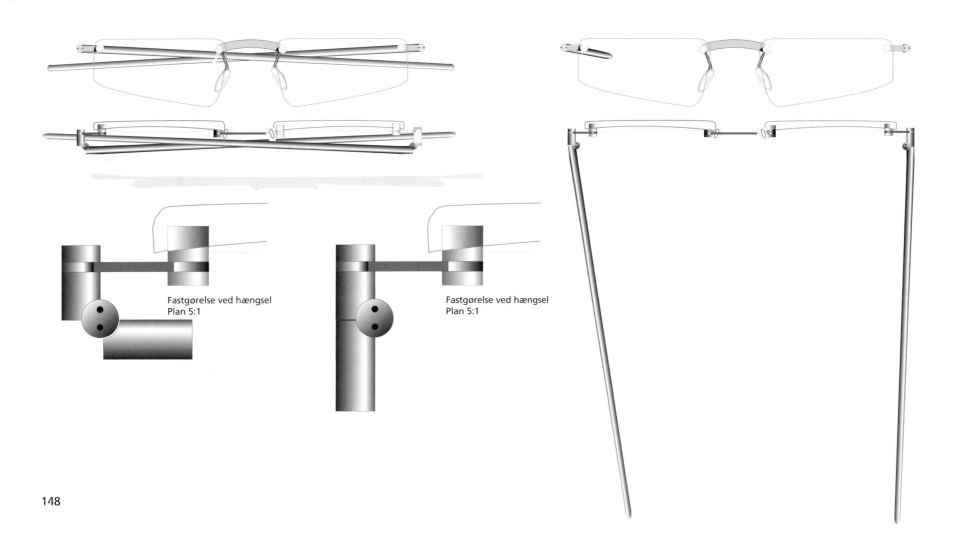

Fastgørelse ved hængsel
Plan 5:1

Fastgørelse ved hængsel
Plan 5:1

Totem for the Copenhagen Metro System
First prize in an international competition

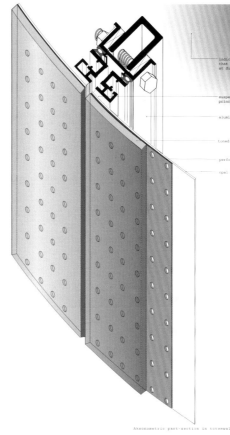

indication of the deep-blue light, that gives the colour a blue glare at dusk

suspension according to the standard principles of structural glazing

aluminium skeleton

toned glasspanel

perforated metallic foil

opal foil

Axonometric part-section in totemwall

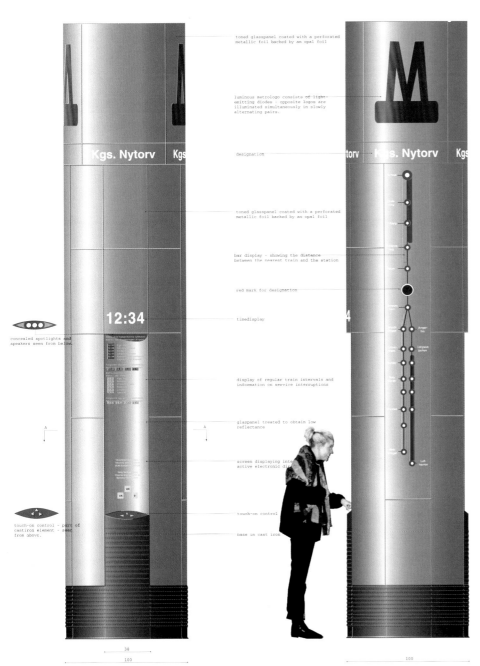

toned glasspanel coated with a perforated metallic foil backed by an opal foil

luminous metrologo consists of light-emitting diodes - opposite logos are illuminated simultaneously in slowly alternating pairs.

designation

toned glasspanel coated with a perforated metallic foil backed by an opal foil

bar display - showing the distance between the nearest train and the station

red mark for designation

timedisplay

concealed spotlights and speakers seen from below.

display of regular train intervals and information on service interruptions

glasspanel treated to obtain low reflectance

screen displaying interactive electronic di...

touch-on control - part of castiron element - seen from above.

touch-on control

base in cast iron

Kgs. Nytorv

12:34

Nytorv   Kgs. Nyt

12:34

service door with hidden lock

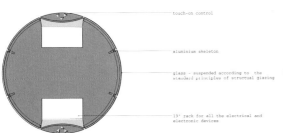

touch-on control

aluminium skeleton

glass - suspended according to the standard principles of structural glazing

19" rack for all the electrical and electronic devices

steelroof

styring of rainwater

service door with hidden lock

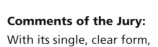

Comments of the Jury:
With its single, clear form, the winner of the competition creates a powerful image, which has the timeless quality that will fit well with Copenhagen's design tradition.

The choice of materials – cast iron and glass – offers a durable, virtually maintenance free solution. The technology for displaying information in the totem was both comprehensive, clear and imaginative.

1

▲ BIBLIOTEK
LIBRARY

◀ MUSEUMSBUTIK
MUSEUM SHOP

BOGGALLERI
BOOK GALLERY

BIBLIOTEK ▶
LIBRARY

2

3

The Danish Museum of Decorative Art, corporate graphic identity program

For the Danish Museum of Decorative Arts in Copenhagen Knud Holscher Industrial Design produced a graphic identity program including signage, directories, guidance brochures, and other related material. A simplified floor plan of the museum is used for the directories located in the entry foyer, as well as for brochures explaining the contents of the various collections.

The signage in the galleries is hung via a system of thin metal wires suspended from ceiling mounted rails. This enables the signs to be changed without damaging the walls in the historically preserved building. The design of the signs makes their method for hanging readily apparent.

Other printed material, the museum's stationery and envelopes for example, have been given a graphic identity analogous to that of the directories and brochures. As an additional part of this corporate identity program two tall glass signs were designed to stand outside the museum's main entry.

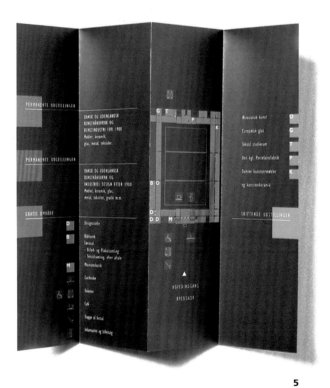

5

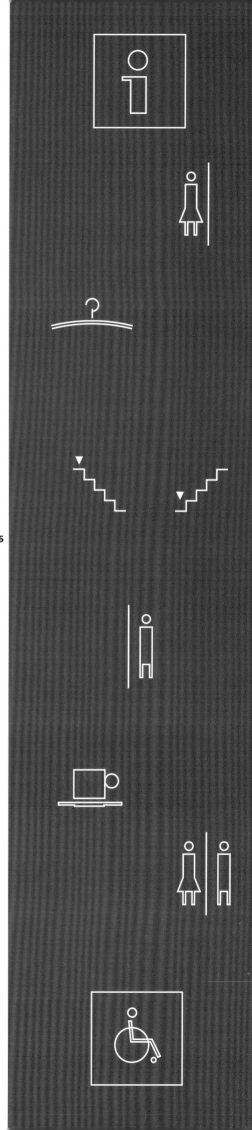

6

4

1. *Sign for use with wire and rail hanging system.*
2. *Detail.*
3. *Museum bag.*
4, 5. *Museum guide and brochures.*
6. *Pictographs.*

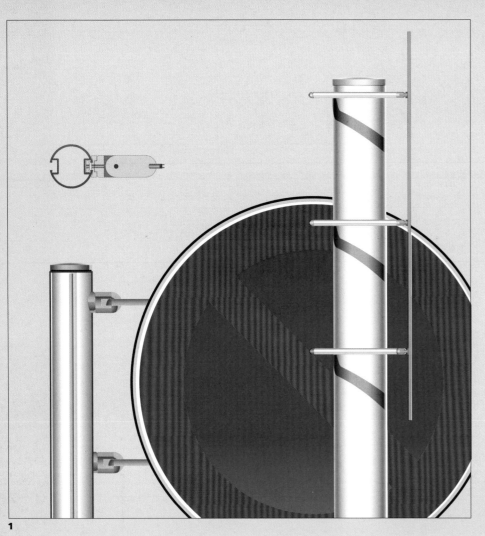

The Danish Road Directorate, road equipment

In 1996, the Danish Director of Highways invited five design firms to take part in a competition for the design of a new system of highway equipment, including street lighting, signage structures, traffic lights, guard rails, benches and tables. The competition called for solutions that were equally durable and beautiful. The series was to be highly crafted and have an overall formal vocabulary that would allow the various objects to be seen as members of the same design family. As many of the components as possible were to be interchangeable. All parts were to be easy to assemble and simple to replace with alterations and maintenance.

1. *Signage boards are constructed of 15 mm honeycomb aluminum. The joints and mast tops are cast elements.*
2. *Drawing illustrating the interrelated design of the signage system's elements.*

1

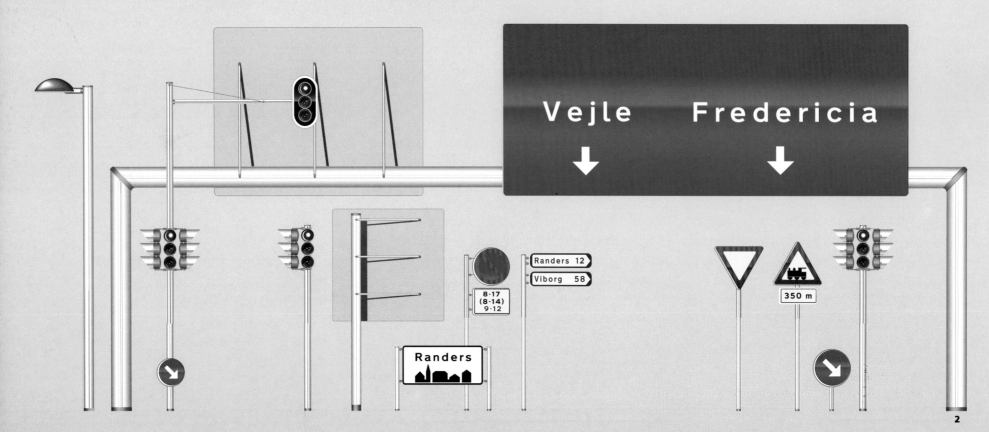

2

Knud Holscher Industrial Design's proposal was selected by the judges because it creatively fulfilled all the complicated demands of the system. Extruded aluminium profiles are used to form the poles and outrigger supports, making them appear as visually elegant as ship masts. The short masts are designed with circular cross sections, while the taller masts are elliptical in profile. The oval cross-section, which gains its strength and efficiency from locating the material thickness at the most static and most appropriate part of the section, is also used for the signage structures that cantilever over the motorways.

It was proposed that the tables and benches be fabricated in cast iron with a surface coating that would protect them from wear and tear while preserving their mark of quality.

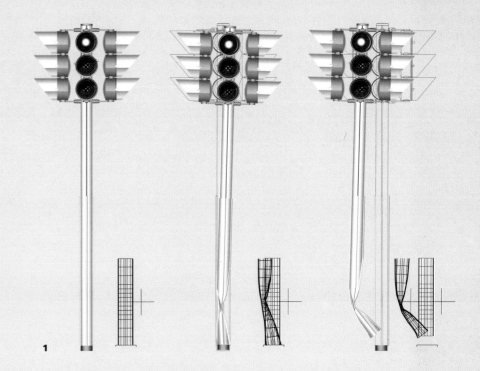

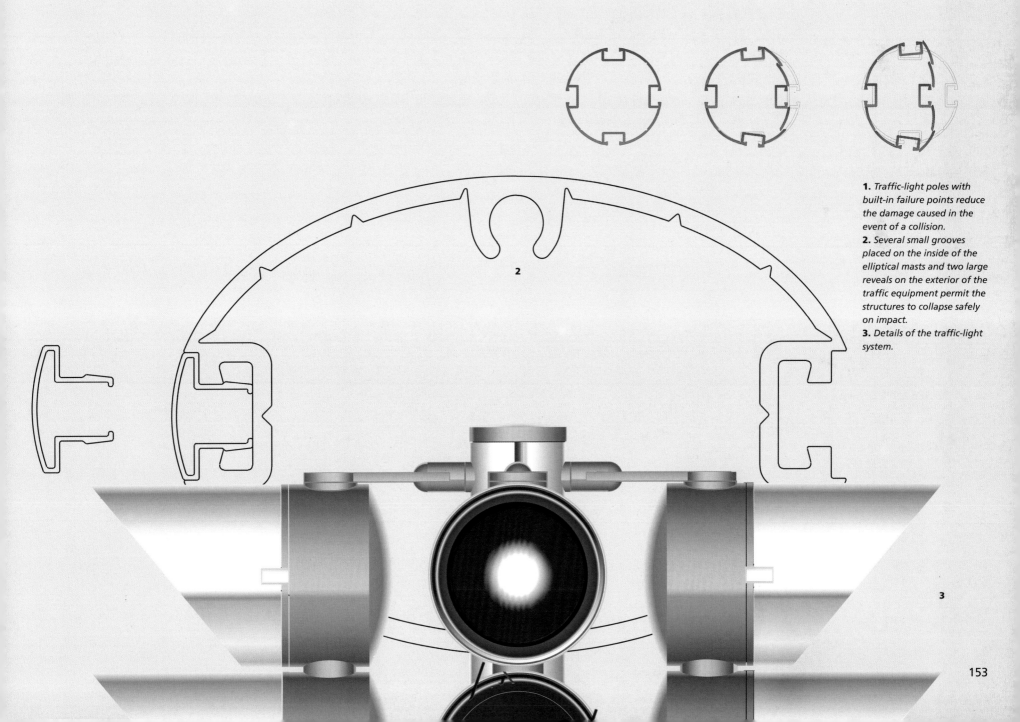

1. Traffic-light poles with built-in failure points reduce the damage caused in the event of a collision.
2. Several small grooves placed on the inside of the elliptical masts and two large reveals on the exterior of the traffic equipment permit the structures to collapse safely on impact.
3. Details of the traffic-light system.

During the system's design development phase, collaborative efforts were established in order to enhance the designs of the various pieces of equipment. Philips was consulted to refine the street lighting while Siemens was used in the design of the traffic lights. "Collision friendly" masts were also created during the developmental stages. The idea behind the pole was a built-in failure point that would collapse safely upon impact. This feature minimizes the damage and injury caused to motor vehicles and users in the event of an accident.

1. *Milewide bench, made of cast iron and elm wood.*
2. *Bus stop shelter with tempered glass sides. Details correspond with other details in the system.*

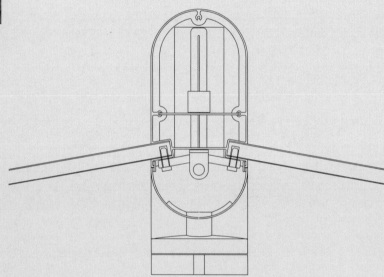

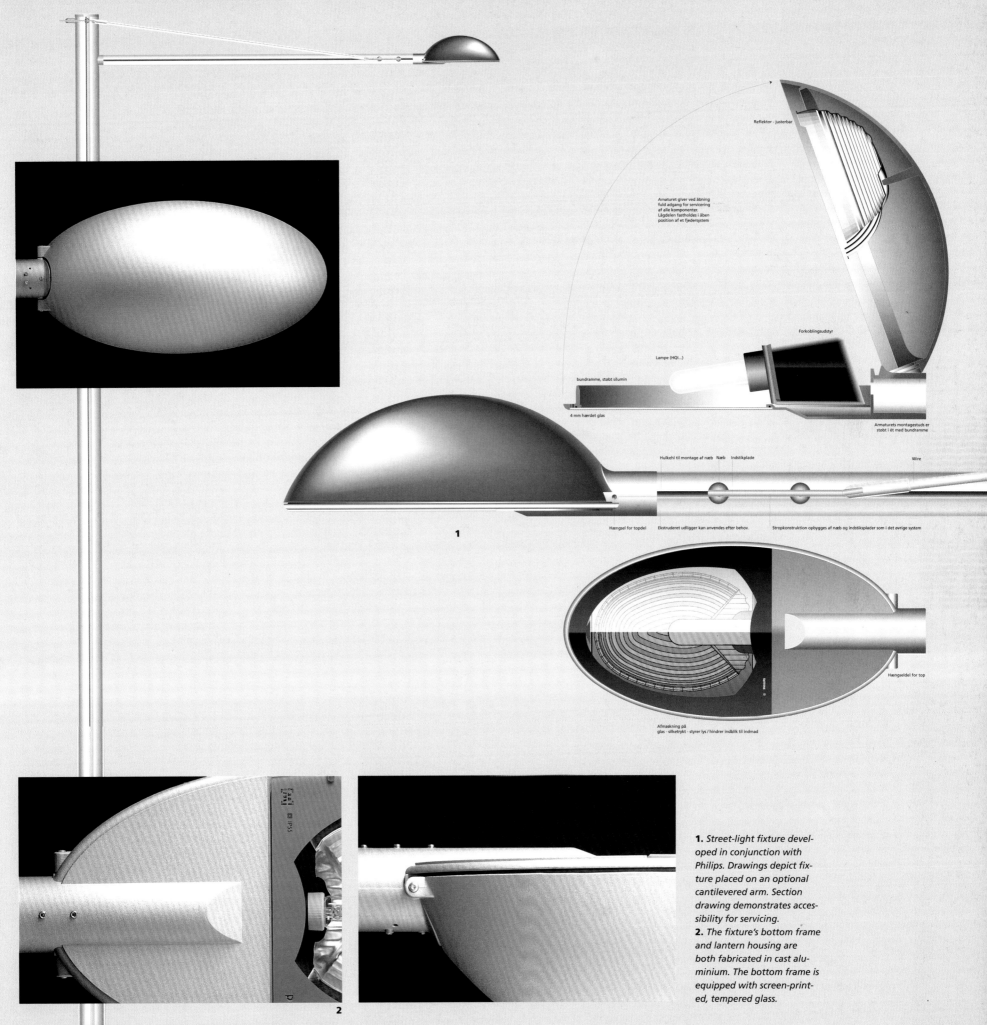

Reflektor - justerbar

Armaturet giver ved åbning
fuld adgang for servicering
af alle komponenter.
Lågdelen fastholdes i åben
position af et fjedersystem

Forkoblingsudstyr

Lampe (HQI...)

bundramme, støbt silumin

4 mm hærdet glas

Armaturets montagestuds er
støbt i ét med bundramme

Hulkehl til montage af næb   Næb   Indstikplade   Wire

Hængsel for topdel   Ekstruderet udligger kan anvendes efter behov.   Stropkonstruktion opbygges af næb og indstiksplader som i det øvrige system

1

Hængseldel for top

Afmaskning på
glas - silketrykt - styrer lys / hindrer indblik til indmad

1. *Street-light fixture developed in conjunction with Philips. Drawings depict fixture placed on an optional cantilevered arm. Section drawing demonstrates accessibility for servicing.*
2. *The fixture's bottom frame and lantern housing are both fabricated in cast aluminium. The bottom frame is equipped with screen-printed, tempered glass.*

2

The Danish Road Directorate, sound screening

In 1996, another competition sponsored by the Director of Highways was held. Four firms were invited to submit proposals for the design of highway sound screening. Despite the fact that the competition targeted a specific stretch of highway in Bispeengbuen, bordering a densely developed residential area, the final solution was to be suited for a more general application to a diversity of roadway conditions.

The competition brief required a sound absorption coefficient of at least 8 dB in relation to the closest façades. The jury set a great deal of emphasis on the aesthetic quality of the screening and on its ability to integrate into both urban and rural settings. The sound screening was to be adaptable to a variety of different terrain conditions, as well as commensurate with local regulations regarding colour, reflectivity, and transparency. The competition called for a system that was quick, easy, and safe to erect. It was also to be possible for other highway equipment to be mounted to the screening if the situation should arise. Finally, the design was to be impact safe, i.e. present the least possible danger in the case of an accident. Any damaged parts were to be easily replaced.

1

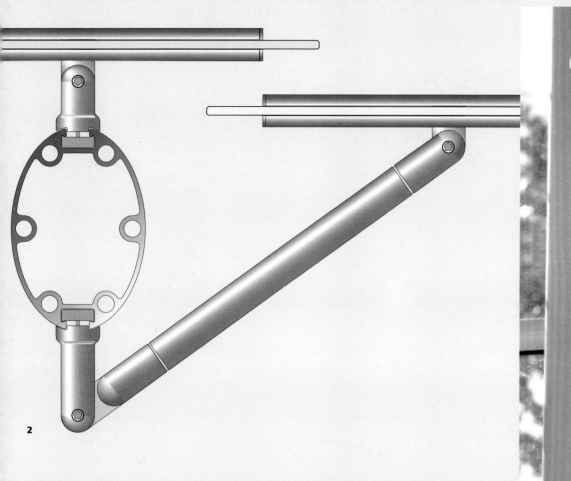

2

During the judging process, the estimated production price was taken into consideration in such a manner that a higher initial cost was accepted if the design was of a high quality that would reduce the costs of maintenance over time.

The jury selected the proposal from Knud Holscher Industrial Design as superior to the others because, among other reasons, it fulfilled the complicated needs of the program using the least number of components. The system is able to accommodate effortlessly both horizontal and vertical movements in the routing line.

1. *View of the sound screening.*
2–4. *The sound screening details are designed with concern for maintenance and repair.*

3

It is an elegant design that relates to the firm's design for highway equipment. The screening's structural elements are fabricated in extruded aluminium. After consulting the Ornithology Society, the overlapping glass plates forming the sound screens were equipped with horizontal stripes to hinder birds from flying into their surfaces.

4

1

Railway station, DSB

In 1996, the Building Department of the Danish State Railways requested that Knud Holscher Industrial Design develops a proposal for the design and layout of new platform appurtenances for its S-train stations. The intent of this design renovation was, among other things, to increase passengers' security and peace of mind by improving the overall clarity of the platform layout. At the same time, the design was to be simple to produce and easy to maintain.

A steel plated column element serves as one of the major components of the design. In addition to supporting the platform's roof structure, the columns also provide built-in lighting, ticket machines, and other such functional elements.

The simple form and the robust materials of all the platform appurtenances can withstand most forms of vandalism. However, in the event of more serious destruction, the

modular design of the system makes it relatively easy to replace any damaged components.

2

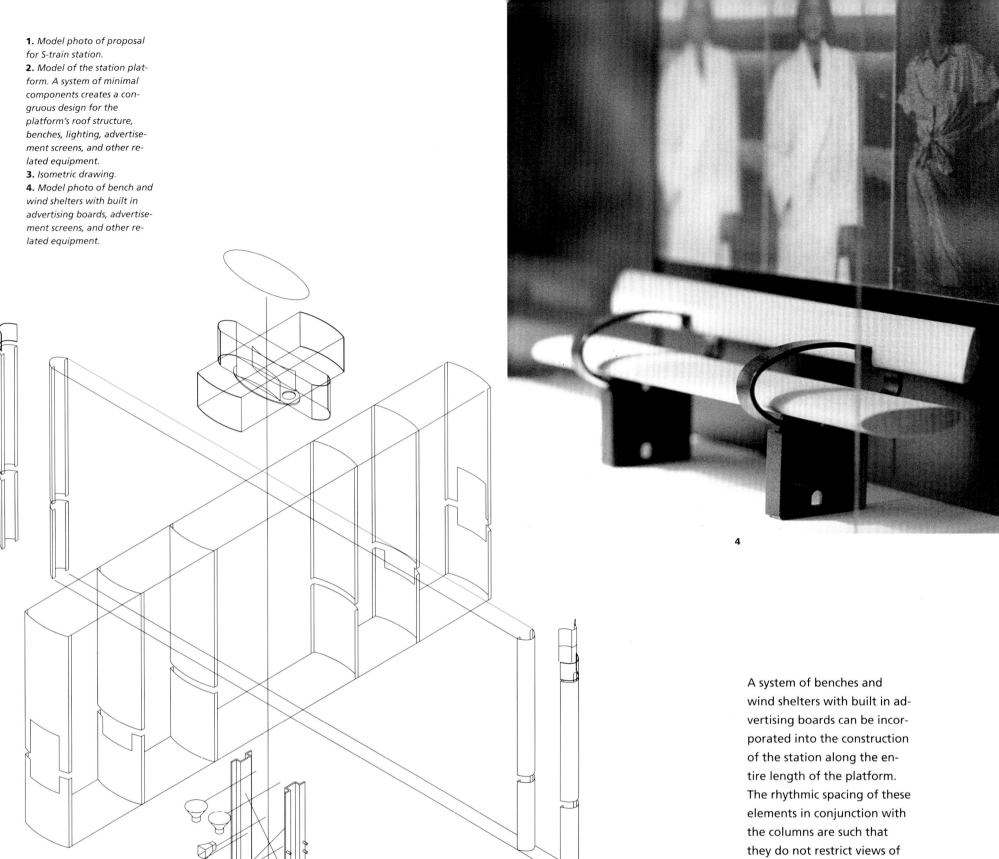

1. *Model photo of proposal for S-train station.*
2. *Model of the station platform. A system of minimal components creates a congruous design for the platform's roof structure, benches, lighting, advertisement screens, and other related equipment.*
3. *Isometric drawing.*
4. *Model photo of bench and wind shelters with built in advertising boards, advertisement screens, and other related equipment.*

4

3

A system of benches and wind shelters with built in advertising boards can be incorporated into the construction of the station along the entire length of the platform. The rhythmic spacing of these elements in conjunction with the columns are such that they do not restrict views of the approaching trains and surrounding context.

The structure of the bench is cast iron, while the seat and back support are of laminated wood.

The project has not been executed to date.

159

1. *Exhibition seen from the first floor balcony.*
2. *Plan of the exhibition.*
3. *Exhibition details seen from the first floor balcony.*
4. *Exhibition seen from the first floor balcony. On display are an AP waste water pump designed by Grundfos, lavatory and water closet models in sanitary porcelain by Knud Holscher Industrial Design, and a solar panel system developed in concert by the architecture firm, Domus and the engineering firm, N&R Consult.*

1

2

Paustian, exhibition

The furniture firm, Paustian, is housed in a building erected in 1987 based on drawings by Jørn, Jan and Kim Utzon. Various exhibitions with themes relating to the utilization of industrial design products are often held in the space. In 1996, The Danish National Bank's Anniversary Fund arranged an exhibition entitled "People, water and design". Knud Holscher Industrial Design was in charge of the exhibition's design. The firm's own work as well as the work of designers Ole Palsby, Christian Bjørn, and Ole Søndergaard was to be exhibited.

The displayed objects related to three themes: water and gastronomy, water and the environment, and water and the body. The industrial design products on display ranged from kitchenware to sanitary porcelain and from diving equipment to waste water pumps. The exhibition was a documentation of Danish design's coherence to the solution of practical assign-ments in everyday situations. It demonstrated how Danish design is usually based on immediate, concrete problems existing in the built environment.

The exhibition was an attractive transient design, a minimalist composition of steel beams and tempered glass plates in variegated formations.

3

4

1

2

3

Munch, office furniture

Through a series of ongoing conceptual investigations in exchange with the furniture company, Fritz Hansen, Knud Holscher developed an intelligent office furniture system for Munch Furniture. The system is for customers who demand quality and aesthetic refinement in the workplace.

The unique form of the table legs is just one of the many special features of this furniture series. They are fabricated in extruded aluminium c-sections, which provide space for concealing almost all general lighting and telecommunication wiring. The legs also contain fittings to accommodate the stable attachment of a secondary, pivoting desktop and other similar elements. The corners of the components can be joined via square tubes with RHS profiles. These tubes also serve to support the desktops, and together with the corner create an extremely rigid desk. Just as in the design of the table legs, the corner connections are designed so that the wiring and cabling

needs of the workstation can be collected and hidden in the structure bracing the desktop surface.

The desktop structure and the cast corners are in a dark grey colour and the legs are of anodized aluminium. The table is appropriate for use as both an executive desk and a standard computer workstation.

A very simple and elegant storage system was also designed in relation to the desking components. Bookcases and cabinets are available in three modular heights and one standard width. The units can be combined freely in response to the different needs and demands of each individual workstation. This office furniture system is suited for progressive professions such as law and accountancy, as well as for the administrative divisions of architecture and advertising firms etc.

opstalt

plan

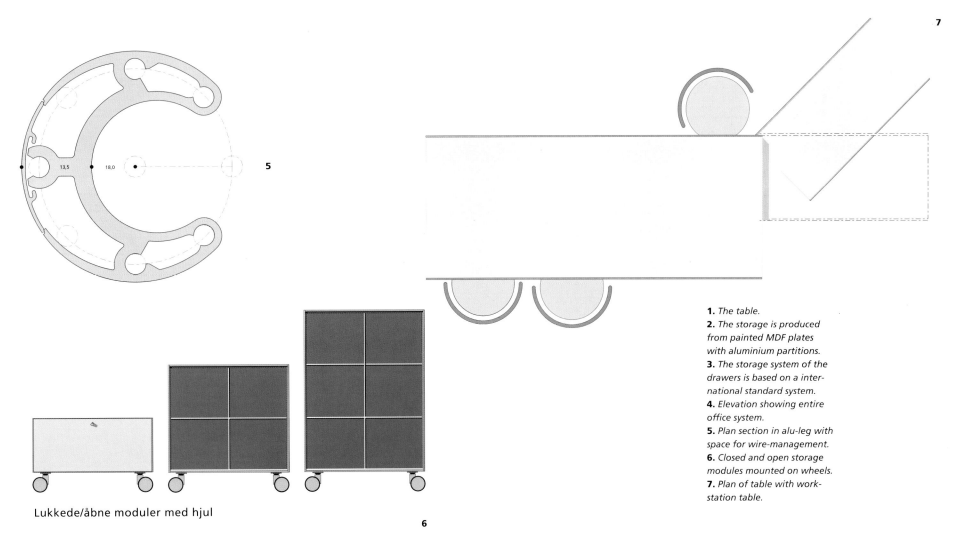

13,5   18,0

5

Lukkede/åbne moduler med hjul

6

1. *The table.*
2. *The storage is produced from painted MDF plates with aluminium partitions.*
3. *The storage system of the drawers is based on a international standard system.*
4. *Elevation showing entire office system.*
5. *Plan section in alu-leg with space for wire-management.*
6. *Closed and open storage modules mounted on wheels.*
7. *Plan of table with workstation table.*

4

7

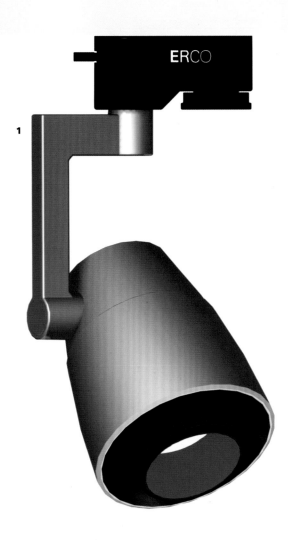

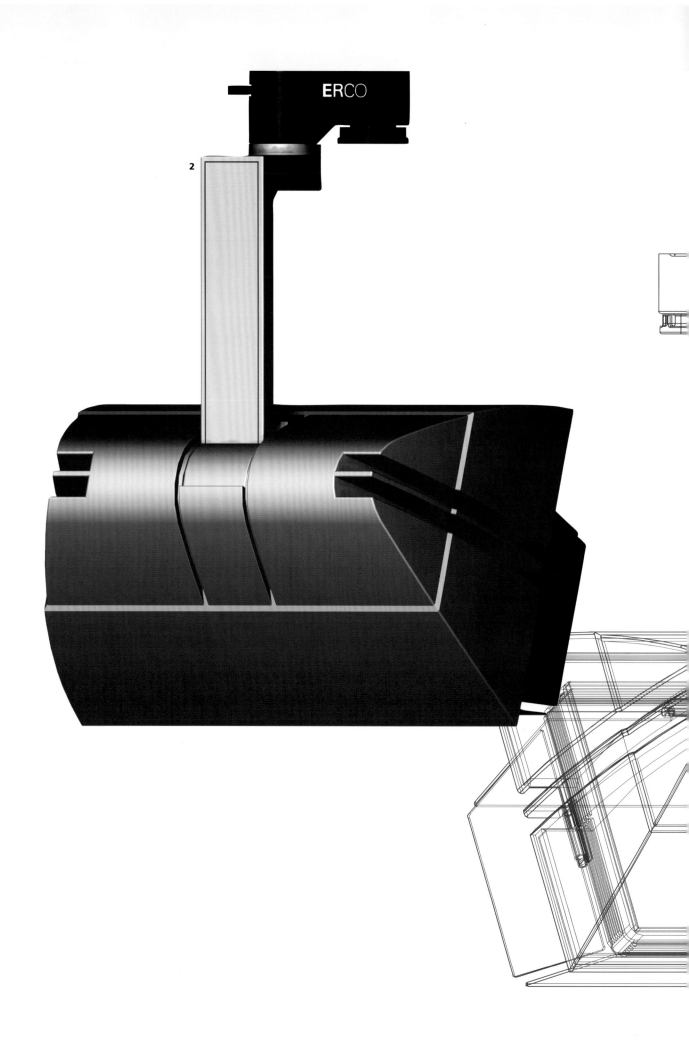

ERCO, Jilly

Computer generated drawings for a series of spot lights for Erco. The different light sources varies in size and heat output.

The flood lightfixture above needs cooling ribs, which becomes part of the design expression.

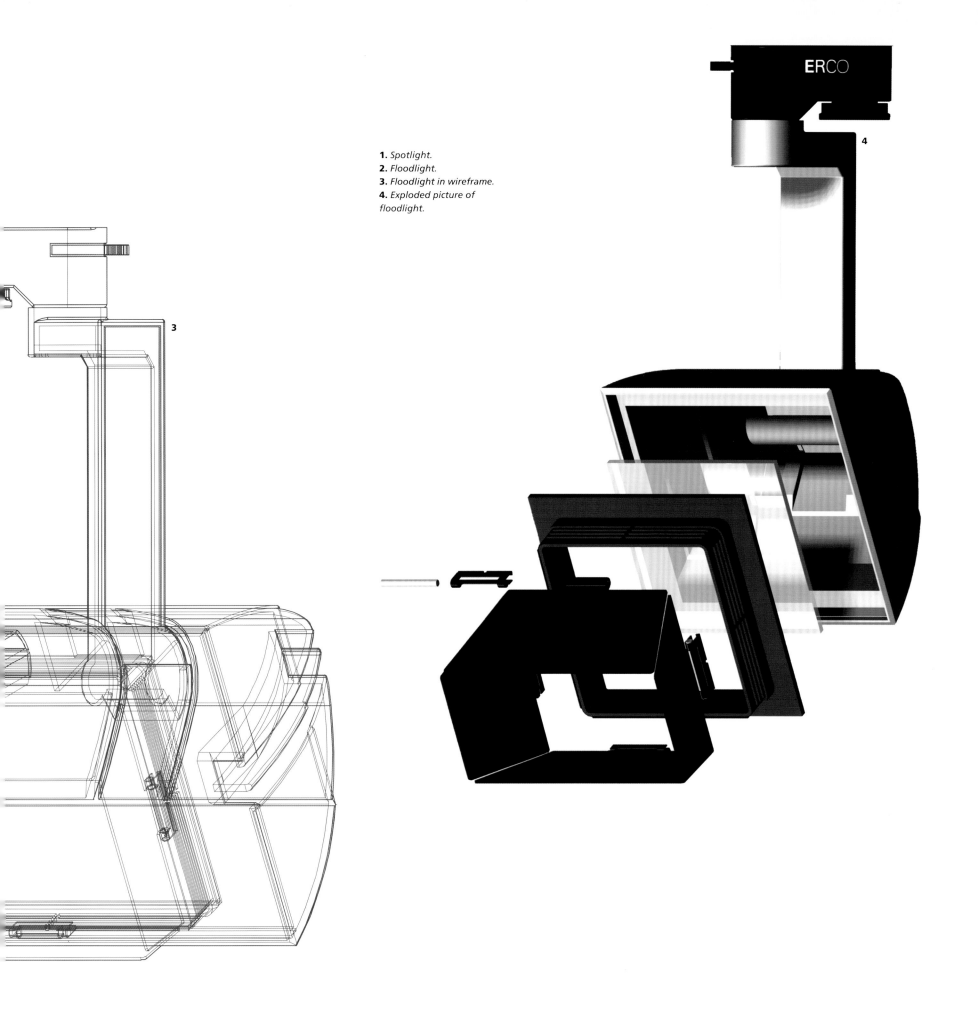

1. *Spotlight.*
2. *Floodlight.*
3. *Floodlight in wireframe.*
4. *Exploded picture of floodlight.*

ERCO

3

4

Knud Holscher's office, Copenhagen

The office of Knud Holscher Industrial Design is housed in an old industrial building dating from the 1930s. The reinforced concrete structure was designed by the American architect, Albert Kahn, and originally functioned as an automobile assembly plant for General Motors. During the last few decades, a Danish-owned factory producing electronic components occupied the building. Today, the building is home to several smaller companies working within the design, photo, and film industries. Knud Holscher has put the building's unique architectural character to use in creating a highly functional and aesthetically refined studio environment.

When Knud Holscher Industrial Design took over the third floor, it was a raw, dilapidated factory space. As part of the renovation and planning of the studio, a new wood floor was laid over the existing concrete floor. This created both a visual continuity and a concealment space (between the two floors) for of the numerous electrical wires and computer cables needed to service the office. The peripheral walls of the space, were left for the most part, in their original condition. However, three glass boxes have been inserted into the centre of the space to define the conference rooms and a reference library. Although it was a directive from the fire inspector initially that the walls be constructed of glass, it was pure architectonic innovation that

1. *View of the studio space seen from the entry area.*
2. *Detail view of the building.*
3. *The conference rooms have been designed as glass boxes equipped with sliding doors.*

ensured that the visual impression of the space was preserved. Entering the space today, the feeling of a workshop still exists. Light and transparency serve to promote the type of interaction that is the basis of the firm's creative endeavors.

One of the numerous interior details of interest is the design of the spacious cabinet units. They are created from the old, stainless steel shelves that were left behind by the previous tenant. The original metal shelves are now concealed behind sliding doors that act as screens or walls within the space. The cabinet doors are painted in charcoal grey, while the walls are of a light grey tone. Within these surroundings it is easy to sense how an exceptional design harmonize with such an exceptional industrial environment.

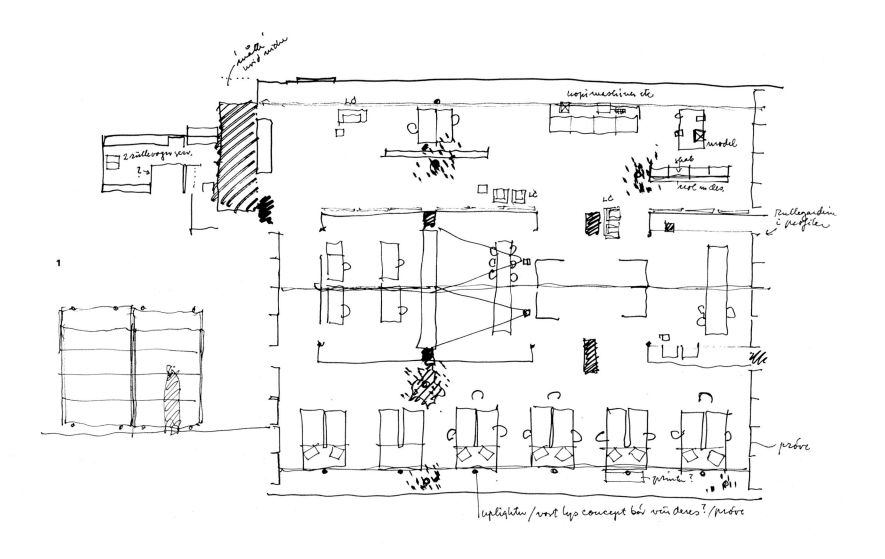

1

2   3

1. *Floor plan sketch of the studio layout.*
2. *Exhibition of the firm's previous design projects.*
3. *Handcrafted, African artifacts juxtaposed in relation to industrial design objects.*
4. *Whilst arranging a new studio space within the old factory locale, as much of the original character of the building was preserved as possible. In order to maintain the open plan, transparent glass boxes have been used to enclose the conference rooms, material library, and other special functions.*
5. *The design office is located in a factory building dating from the 1930s.*

Part 8

KHR AS

(1985)

(1998)

Knud Holscher Industrial Design

Associates since 1996

Jens Christian Larsen

Per Kristian Dahl

Anders Brix Pedersen

Staff

Jette Møller Sørensen

John Nielsen

Birgitte Redin

Karina Mose

Jens Fugl

Friederike Faller

Stig Myler

Michael Sebber Colfelt

Photo credits

Club Manhattan

90, 91

ERCO

138, 139, 140, 141

Facit io

96, 97, 98, 99, 100

GH form

154

Marianne Grøndahl

3

Graae & Bangsbo

158, 159, 160, 172

Knud Holscher

106, 109, 110, 111, 112, 113, 114, 115,
116, 117, 118, 119, 124, 125, 126, 127,
156, 157, 160(1), 161

IFÖ:

46, 47

H. H. Johansen

84, 144

Jens Christian Larsen

41, 89(4), 130

Ole Meyer

37, 40, 73, 74, 75, 92, 120, 121, 122,
123, 133(2), 142, 143, 146, 150, 151,
166, 167, 168, 169

Royal Copenhagen

88

Jørgen Strüwing

132, 133(1), 134, 135, 136, 137, 145,
155, 162

Henning Thygesen

16, 17, 18, 19, 21, 22, 23, 24, 26, 27,
28, 29, 30, 31, 35, 36, 42, 43, 44, 45,
48, 49, 50, 51, 54, 55, 56, 57, 60, 51,
62, 64, 65, 66, 67,68, 69, 70, 71, 72, 76,
77, 78, 79, 82, 83, 84, 85, 87, 94, 102,
103, 172

Associates in architecture

The University of Odense

1976

KHR AS

The University of Uleåborg

1970

KHR AS

The University of Jyväskylä

1970

KHR AS

The University of Odense, built project

1976

KHR AS

Svend Axelsson

Erik Sørensen

Knud Holscher's own house, Holte

1971

Royal Theatre, Copenhagen

1978

Svend Axelsson

The Town Hall Square

1980

KHR AS

Svend Axelsson

Jægersborg Centre

1990

KHR AS

Svend Axelsson

Erik Sørensen

Kurt Schou

Copenhagen's harbour

1982

KHR AS

Svend Axelsson

Cultural Centre in Neumünster

1991

KHR AS

Svend Axelsson

Swimming centre in Farum

1981

KHR AS

Svend Axelsson

The Copenhagen Airport, Domestic Terminal

1991

KHR AS

Svend Axelsson

Erik Sørensen

The Copenhagen Airport, multi-storey car park

1991

KHR AS

Svend Axelsson

Erik Sørensen

The Copenhagen Airport, Finger B

1987

KHR AS

Svend Axelsson

Erik Sørensen

Unicon Concrete

1989

KHR AS

Svend Axelsson

Jan Søndergård

Bahrain Civic Centre, Bahrain

1989

KHR AS

Svend Axelsson

Erik Sørensen

The Danish Pavilion, Expo '92, Seville

1992

KHR AS

Svend Axelsson

Jan Søndergård

Knud Holscher's vacation house

1994

Knud Holscher's office, Copenhagen

1995

Per Kr. Dahl

Anders Brix Pedersen

Associates in design

Modric

1966

Alan Tye

po inventar

1976

Gert Edstrand

Participating staff

The people listed here are among
those who have worked in the
office and assisted in the projects
in this book.

Architecture

Niels Bruun

Jan Bülow

Kresten Bloch

Jan Christiansen

Jens Clementsen

Ole Gjølberg

Jørgen Hansen

Bente Vestergaard Høj

Karsten Høyer

Vivi Iversen

Henrik Lading

Steffen Larsen

Svend René Larsen

Torben Møller Larsen

Søren Lund

Brian Gwilyn Martin

Jens Bryrup Mikkelsen

John Nielsen

Ulla-Helene Færgemann Nielsen

Torben Nagel

Ove Neumann

Dan Reese

Lone Scavenius

Kurt Schou

Finn Selmer

Ib Skotte

Jan Søndergaard

Erik Sørensen

Niels Pinholt

Gudni Pålsson

Design

Per Buchard

Erik Bystrup

Michael Sebber Colfelt

Per Kristian Dahl

Friederike Faller

Jens Christian Larsen

Jesper Lund

Jens Fugl

Leif Hagerup

Phillip Bro Ludwigsen

Peter Mortensen

Karina Mose

John Nielsen

Anders Brix Pedersen

Birgitte Redin

Jens Rølling

Carsten Schmidt

Gunilla Svendsen

Jette Møller Sørensen

Stig Myler

Hanne Uhlig

Kenneth Warnke

Sten Zinck

Curriculum vitae

Born

1930.

Nationality

Danish.

Education

School of Architecture, The Royal Danish
Academy of Fine Arts, Copenhagen,
Denmark.

Languages

English, German.

Professional Societies

Association of Academic Architects (MAA).
Federation of Danish Architects (DAL).
Industrial Designers Denmark (IDD).

Recent Positions

1999, Establishment of Holscher Associates,
Architects MAA.
1995, Establishment of Knud Holscher
Industriel Design.
1994 and 1968–1988, Professor, School of
Architecture, The Royal Danish Academy
of Fine Arts, Copenhagen, Denmark.
1968, Partner, Krohn & Hartvig Rasmussen,
Architects and Planners. Shareholder and
member of the board since the firm's trans-
transformation into a joint-stock corpora-
tion – KHR A/S Architects – in 1988.

Professional Experiences

1998

Morsø Iron Foundry A/S, Denmark; wood
burning stove.
Munch Furniture A/S; Holscher Office
Furniture Series for Munch Furniture A/S,
Denmark.
ERCO; Series 4.
1st prize in a competition for 'traffic totems'
for the Copenhagen Metro.
1st prize in an international competition for
bus shelters in Århus, Denmark.
(Collaboration with AFA JCDecaux, Paris)
Competition, DSB (Danish State Railways)
Information Stands.
Design for a backstage building for Østre
Gasværk Theatre.
Award form The Cultural Foundation of
Copenhagen for the Østre Gasværk Theatre
design.

1997

1st prize in Copenhagen's Urban Renewal
Competition for environmentally sound
building components.
Ridderkors af Dannebrogsordenen Award.

1996

Philips A/S; highway appurtenances.
Siemens A/S; bus timetable and information
boards.
Cultural Capital '96 Exhibition at Paustian,
sponsored by the National Bank Foundation.
1st prize in the Metropolitan Traffic
Association's design competition for sound
screening.
1st prize in the Metropolitan Traffic
Association's design competition for highway
appurtenances.
Jury member, The Brunel Award, DSB,
international design competition for railway
architecture.
Jury member, The International Design Award
of Baden-Württemberg, Germany.
Design of Road Sign System for the
Metropolitan Traffic Association.
Project for metropolitan stations, DSB,
(Danish State Railways).

1995

Graphic Identity Program for the Danish
Museum of Decorative Arts.
"Honourable Mention", diploma from the
Society for the Beautification of the Capital
for bus stop shelter design.
The European Solar Prize 1995 for the
Bruntland Centre Denmark.
Swedish Form-95 Design Award for IFÖ
Ceranova Series.
Bahrain National Museum is nominated for
the Aga Khan Award for a second time.

1994

1st prize in a competition for Odense
University's Faculty of Natural Sciences
building.
Nominated for the Mies van der Rohe Award.
Professor, Design Institute, The Royal Danish
Academy of Fine Arts.
Nominated for the Japan International
Design Award.

1993

Jury Member, Museum of Modern Art
Competition, Helsinki.
3rd prize in an international architectural
competition for The Royal Danish Library,
Copenhagen.
August Perret Award for Applied Technology
in Architecture.
Design consultant to The Øresund Link.
Award of Honour, The Danish National Bank.
C. F. Hansen Medal, The Royal Danish
Academy of Fine Arts.

1992

Invited to display works in an exhibition in
Helsinki, Finland as one of five "Nordic
Masters".
Architect of the Danish Pavilion at EXPO '92
in Seville, Spain.
Award-winning proposal for "Copenhagen
Waste System" competition.
Nykredit Award for the Danish Pavilion,
Seville, Spain.
European Design Award for Unicon,
Denmark.
Nominated for the Mies van der Rohe Award
for the Danish Pavilion, Seville, Spain.
Design consultant to Rosti, Denmark;
household storage units.
Design consultant to Fritz Hansen A/S,
Denmark; office furniture.

1991

Diploma from the Society for the
Beautification of the Capital for Copenhagen
Airport's Finger B extension and Domestic
Terminal.

1990

1st prize in a competition for a multi-storey
parking garage for the Copenhagen Airport.
Design for an office furniture series for
Design Funktion AB (Facit), Sweden.
Jury Member, architectural competition in
Oslo, Norway for Olav Thon A/S.
Jury Member, urban renewal competition.
ERCO Leuchten, Germany; lighting fixtures.
OCLI, USA and Scotland; computer monitor
filters.

1989

"Betonelementprisen 1989" (The Concrete Panel Award) for the Finger B extension to the Copenhagen Airport, and for Unicon Beton's main office in Roskilde, Denmark.
1st prize in an EC-competition for low-energy office buildings.
Design for Højgaard & Schulz A/S's main office building in Herlev, Denmark.
1st prize in the competition for the Danish Pavilion at EXPO '92 in Seville, Spain.
Jury member, airport competition, Oslo, Norway.
Union of German Architects (BDA) Award for the design of a community centre in Neumünster, Germany.

1988

1st prize in a competition for a gasometer, HNG (Metropolitan Natural Gas).
Invited to display works in Charlottenborg's "Autumn 1988 Exhibition", Copenhagen, Denmark.
Coloplast A/S; colostomy bag.
Blücher Metalvarer; grill series.
Nordplan; compact shelving.
Paustian; letterbox.
Tron-Pax ApS; illumination management system for ILS.
IFÖ Mörrum; stainless steel sink.
Club Manhattan series purchased by The Danish State Art Foundation.
Design for Jægersborg Centre.
Design for the Copenhagen Airport Domestic Terminal.

1987

1st prize in the Stadion Denmark, competition for a football stadium.

1986

1st prize in an architectural competition for Unicon Beton's administration building, Roskilde, Denmark.
Frankfurt Messe Design Award for Club Manhattan series.
2nd prize in an architectural competition for town and traffic planning, Lyngby Town Centre, Denmark.
Design manual for the Municipality of Herlev, Copenhagen.
Design for the Copenhagen Airport Domestic Terminal.
Visiting Professor, Universities of Adelaide, Sidney and Melbourne, Australia.
Exhibition of Club Manhattan series at the Stuttgart Design Centre.

1985

1st prize in an invited competition sponsored by the Copenhagen Airport for the design of an office building.
Design for Finger B extension for the Copenhagen Airport.
Dampa; ceilings and walls.
Royal Copenhagen; various design commissions.
Nordisk Solar; lighting.
Nordisk Solar; catalogue, PR, etc.
Dansk Pressalit; toilet seats.
Stone Art, Belgium; Club Manhattan.
1st prize in an invited competition for the Lyngby Stadium Sports Centre.
1st prize in an architectural competition for Køge Swimming Centre.

1984

Introduction of the IFÖ Aqua sanitary porcelain line into the Scandinavian market
1st prize in the Dampa Design Competition for an integrated ceiling component system.
1st prize in a competition for beds, sponsored by Illums Bolighus, Copenhagen, Denmark.
1st prize in a competition for Strandmarkshave Nursing Home in Hvidovre, Denmark.
1st prize in a competition for a retail building in connection with Østerport Station, Copenhagen, Denmark.

1983

Stringline wins awards at the Scandinavian Lighting Fair, as well as the Göteborg and Hanover Fairs.
Stringline is placed on a permanent exhibition at Die Neue Sammlung, Staatliches Museum für angewandte Kunst, Munich, Germany.
1st prize in a conceptual design competition for elderly domiciles and nursing care facilities in Ikast, Denmark.
1st prize in an invited competition for the Danish Post and Telegraph Service, CTVLAB, Tåstrup, Denmark.
Design for a combined residential and retail centre, Jægersborg Allé.
Work for the Copenhagen Airport, Kastrup, Denmark.
Exhibition of kitchenware designed for Georg Jensen Sølvsmedie A/S at the Philadelphia Museum of Art.
3rd prize in a competition sponsored by The Royal Copenhagen Porcelain Factory.

1982

1st prize in an architectural competition for extensions to the firm of Brüel & Kjærs in Nærum, Denmark.

1981

Design for a guest palace in Bahrain.
Awarded the K. V. Engelhardt's Memorial Grant for design work.
1st prize in an invited competition for a town hall in Næstved, Denmark.
Design for a civic centre and national museum in Bahrain.
3rd prize in an architectural competition for a technical university in Berlin.

1980

Design for private residences in Geneva and Cannes.

1979

1st prize in an invited architectural competition for a sports centre in Grenå, Denmark.
Member, of the Danish Design Council.
1st prize in a competition for a hall for racket games in Herlev, Denmark.
"Træprisen" Danish Architectural Award, (prize for the creative use of wood in building constructions).
Commended prize in an architectural competition for the planning of a town-hall square in Odense, Denmark.
1st prize in an architectural competition for a community centre in Neumünster, Germany.
1st prize in a project competition for the Royal Theatre, Copenhagen, Denmark.
Design consultant to Toni fittings A/S; T-line fitting series.

1978

1st prize in an architectural competition for a public swimming centre in Værløse, Denmark.
1st prize in a competition for two schools in Aalborg, Denmark.
Commended prize in an architectural competition for the master plan and renovation Kokkedal Manor, Denmark.
Award in a conceptual design competition for the development of glass-wool sandwich panel constructions.
PEVO A/S; steel doorframe.
Joint 1st prize in a conceptual design competition for the Royal Theatre, Copenhagen, Denmark.

1977

Prize in an international competition for an office building in Vienna, Austria.
Design for JOS University, Nigeria, master plan after competition.
The Autumn Exhibition at Charlottenbor, Copenhagen, Denmark.

1976

1st prize in an invited competition for a swimming centre in Lyngby, Denmark.
1st prize in an invited competition for a sports centre in Lundtofte, Denmark.
1st prize in an invited competition for a skating rink in Herlev, Denmark.
Joint 1st prize in an architectural competition for a swimming centre in Greve, Denmark.
Award in an international architectural competition for Munkebo School, Denmark.
Design for SIB concrete girder system for Højgaard & Schultz A/S Contractors, Denmark.
Design consultant to Perstorp AB, Sweden; lavatory partition wall.
Design consultant to IFÖ Sanitär AB, Sweden; Aqua sanitary porcelain line.
Design consultant to H. F. Belysning, Denmark; stainless steel lighting fixtures.

1975

Commended prize in a competition for Aalborg University Centre, Denmark.
Commended prize in a competition for Haderslev University Centre, Denmark.

1974

Design consultant to Georg Jensen Sølvsmedie A/S; production of various designs.
1st prize in a competition for energy-saving housing.

1973

Architectural collaboration with Svend Axelsson.
2nd prize in an architectural competition for the Aalborg Central Library, Denmark.
Design exhibition sponsored by Danish Handicrafts, Sønderborg, Denmark.

1972

IDD Design Exhibition at Nikolaj Plads, Copenhagen, Denmark.
Design of own residence in Holte, Denmark.

1971

2nd prize in a German competition for a technical university in Munich.

1970

Awarded the Eckersberg Medal by The Royal Danish Academy of Fine Arts.
Award in a Scandinavian competition for the University of Jyväskylä, Finland.

1969

1st prize from the Guild of Architectural Ironmongers for the Syncronol sign system. (Collaboration with Alan Tye.)

1968

Appointed Professor at the School of Architecture, The Royal Danish Academy of Fine Arts, Copenhagen, Denmark.

1967

Award in a Scandinavian competition for the development of the island of Hven, Sweden, into a holiday centre.
Award for the University of Uleåborg, Finland.

1966

1st prize in a competition for a sports centre in Ikast, Denmark.
1st prize from the Guild of Architectural Ironmongers for the Modric fitting series. (Collaboration with Alan Tye.)
Awarded the Theophilos Hansen Travel Grant.
1st prize in a British competition for office sign system. (Collaboration with Alan Tye.)
Partner, Krohn & Hartvig Rasmussen, Architects and Planners.
1st prize in a Scandinavian competition for a university in Odense, Denmark.

1964–68

Teacher, (Assistant to Professor E. Chr. Sørensen), School of Architecture, The Royal Danish Academy of Fine Arts, Copenhagen, Denmark.

1963

Award in an international competition for sanitary equipment. (Collaboration with Alan Tye.)
Award in a competition for a public school in Søllerød, Denmark.
Award in a Scandinavian competition for a new town quarter in Herning, Denmark.

1960–64

Associate architect with Professor Arne Jacobsen. Work as project architect for the design of St Catherine's College, Oxford, England. (2 years residence in England.)

1959–60

Employed by Professor Arne Jacobsen. Team member on competitions for a school in Rødovre, Denmark and the WHO (World Health Organization) Centre in Geneva.

1958–60

Teacher (Assistant to Professor E. Chr. Sørensen), School of Architecture, The Royal Danish Academy of Fine Arts, Copenhagen, Denmark.

1955–60

Award winning competition proposals:
School in Holstebro, Denmark.
School in Horsens, Denmark.
Single-family housing competition sponsored by a Danish savings bank.

1956–57

Postgraduate student, School of Architecture, The Royal Danish Academy of Fine Arts, Copenhagen, Denmark.

1955

Graduation from the School of Architecture, The Royal Danish Academy of Fine Arts, Copenhagen, Denmark.

Design awards

- ID Prize for d line built-in sanitary panel system, 1999.
- Danish Design Council's Classic Prize for d line, 1999.
- IF Prize, IF Product Design Award for d line built-in sanitary panel system, 1999.
- "The Red Dot Award", Design Zentrum, Nordrhein-Westfalen, for d line cup dispenser, numbers and letters, 1997.
- ID prize for Pictoform Tactile Way-finding System for GH form, 1997.
- IF Prize, IF Product Design Award for d line cup dispenser, 1997.
- "The Red Dot Award", Design Zentrum, Nordrhein-Westfalen, for IFÖ Ceranova Series, 1995.
- "Bundespreis Produktdesign 1994" for Quinta, ERCO.
- IF Prize, IF Product Design Award for Quinta, ERCO, 1993.
- "The Red Dot Award", Design Zentrum, Nordrhein-Westfalen, for Quinta, ERCO, 1993.
- "Ion-Erkenning", Goed Industrieel Ontwerp, Voorjaarsbeurs, Holland for Club Manhattan, 1987.
- "Design Innovationen", Haus Industrieform-Essen for Club Manhattan, 1987.
- IG Prize for d line catalogue, 1987.
- IF Prize, IF Product Design Award for TRIANGLE fluorescent light fixture, 1984.
- ID Prize, for SIB concrete girder system for Højgaard & Schultz A/S Contractors Denmark, 1978.
- IF Prize, IF Product Design Award for d line and light fixture series, 1978.
- ID Prize for the UFO series for Riscanco A/S, 1977.
- ID Prize for d line for Carl F. Petersen, 1975.
- British Design Award for office sign system, 1970.
- British Aluminium Industry Award for the Modric fitting series, 1966. (Collaboration with Alan Tye.) British Design Award for the Modric fitting series, 1966 (Collaboration with Alan Tye.)
- British Design Award for Meridian One, 1965. (Collaboration with Alan Tye.)
- British Design Award for Meridian One, a series of sanitary equipment, 1963. (Collaboration with Alan Tye.)

Epilogue

The creation process is fascinating – from the very first drafts at school to the many real projects completed in later years.

As my teacher and colleague, Professor E. Chr. Sørensen has been essential to my development – and so has the School of Architects.

I have participated in competitions together with Ole Dreyer, Henrik Gormsen and Erik Korshagen; with Erik Bystrup; for Arne Jacobsen; with Alan Tye; for KHR AS and later in the same firm especially with Svend Axelsson but also Jesper Lund and Erik Sørensen.

I am now working in co-operation with my staff in Knud Holscher Industriel Design and notably my associates Anders Brix, Jens Chr. Larsen and Per Kristian Dahl.

All these relationships have contributed to the ongoing education and training which are integral parts of the profession.

My wife Henny has been my partner through all these years, and I am very grateful to her for all her support.